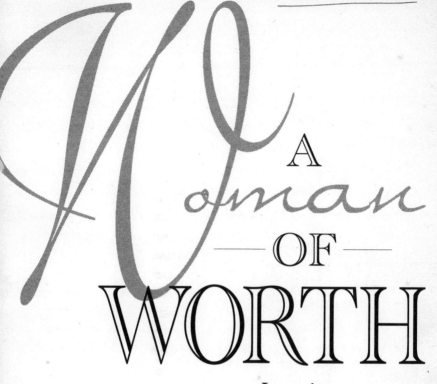

A Woman OF WORTH

*Learning
to live as
a daughter
of the King*

Tamyra Horst

Pacific Press® Publishing Association
Nampa, Idaho
Oshawa, Ontario, Canada

Edited by Glen Robinson
Designed by Michelle Petz
Cover art and background by Image©1996 PhotoDisc, Inc.

Copyright © 1998 by
Pacific Press® Publishing Association
Printed in the United States
All Rights Reserved

Horst, Tamyra, 1961-
     A woman of worth : living as a daughter of the King / Tamyra
Horst.
        p.   cm.
     ISBN 0-8163-1579-5 (alk. paper)
     1. Women—Religious life.   2.   Self-esteem—Religious
aspects—Christianity. 3. Christian life. I. Title.
BV4527.H636   1998
248.8'43—dc21   97-45755
                                                        CIP

98 99 00 01 02 • 5 4 3 2 1

Dedication

This book is dedicated to His other daughters, those who have encouraged me as I've written and grown in Him. Without them, this wouldn't be possible.

To Sue: Your prayers and encouragement have meant so much. I treasure our weekly prayer times and the strength and growth they've brought.

To Tanya: Your friendship is such a source of encouragement and strength. I like that we can be so honest with our struggles and discouragements and rejoice in each other's joys. (And now you can stop asking me, "Are you writing?"—it's done!)

To Mary: I'm so glad that God brought us together as friends and prayer partners. We've shared so much about the struggles of parenting and have learned so much about growing in Him.

To Janet: who has dreamed dreams for me that are bigger than I dared dream. Even at long distance, your friendship and encouragement means so much to me.

To Lilly: A friend with such a love for the Lord, you've taught me much about abiding in Him.

And to my mom, Mary DeVoe: another daughter of His, also a sister of mine, I love you so very much—you're one of my best friends!

Contents

"For you are set apart as a daughter to the Lord your God;
the Lord your God has chosen you to be a daughter for Himself,
a special treasure above all else on the face of the earth.
The Lord did not set His love on you nor choose you
because you were great or important or beautiful or talented,
or because you could accomplish a lot on His behalf,
but because the Lord loves you and He will keep His promises,
the Lord has brought you out with a mighty hand
and redeemed you from sin.
Therefore know that the Lord your God, He is God,
the faithful God who keeps covenant and mercy
for a thousand generations with those who love Him
and keep His commandments."
Deuteronomy 7:6-9, Tami's paraphrase

one

Who Is She?

If you asked people about her, you would get different answers from different people.

Her teachers would tell you that she was a good student. Often the teacher's pet. Always handed in assignments on time. Cooperative, followed rules, listened to authority. Her English teachers would tell you of the creative writing assignments that she handed in. She had a flair for writing. Now *German* was a different subject. . . .

After meeting with her during her senior year, her guidance counselor said, "You have everything going for you." Great grades that came easily. A part-time job. A scholarship and summer job that would completely cover her first year at college. She had been accepted at the only college she had applied to early in her senior year. She had definite plans for her life. Major in English and communications. After graduating, she planned to get a job in human and public relations with a major corporation. She was actively involved in many activities at school—band, chorus, student council, the track team, Future Business Leaders,

Future Medical Careers, Pep Club, German Club. Plus, she was actively involved in her local church youth group.

At the youth group, she participated in everything too. Helping the ladies of the church with missionary breakfasts and Vacation Bible Schools. Listening to other youth talk about their problems with their parents and their dabbling in smoking and drugs. She attended the weekly Bible study for young people called the "Leaders Group." These were young people who had made a commitment to attending the weekly Bible study and were leading out in youth activities, planning, promoting. The adults in the youth group had chosen her to be part of the "Honors Group." This group was chosen from the Leaders Group to be peer leaders and counselors.

Her friends at school would tell you that she was quiet but always willing to help anyone. She laughed and talked with anyone she knew but never really approached new people. She never got in trouble and hung out in the band room during her few study halls. She didn't date but had a number of guys as friends. She worked at the local Howard Johnson's as a waitress and drove a dark blue Chevy. Nothing spectacular. Just your average person.

Her family, of course, loved her. Her brothers counted on her to smooth the way for them with their parents when they got in trouble. Her parents were proud of her, even if they didn't tell her often. Her father always knew that she would make it as a writer one day. He believed in her but was busy providing for a family with five children and a mess of animals. Her mom was proud of how involved she was in school and that she was going to college. She'd be one of the few from their extended family who did. Her mom had often wished she had. Or that she had been more involved in school. Her cousin said, "She's got her head on straight; you don't have to worry about her."

But she did worry. And now as she stood watching her reflection in the mirror, she let the tears flow. She was tired. Tired of trying to measure up, of trying to be what she thought everyone wanted her to be, of trying to please. Her life felt like it was rushing by too fast, and she was caught up in it, whether she liked it or not.

She was a Christian. She had given her life to the Lord when she was about eight years old. She remembered that summer day in her old neighborhood. The Good News Club had come to a neighbor's house and for a week, several teenagers had shared Bible stories and songs. The last afternoon they talked of Jesus and how He loved each one of them just as they were. *Just as I am!* she had thought, *I don't have to compete with my brothers or do everything right.* Too shy to go forward when a call was given for those who wanted to accept Jesus as their Saviour, she had run home and up the stairs to her room. Kneeling beside the white bedspread, surrounded by the turquoise and pink flowered walls, she had asked Jesus into her life. It was a decision she had never regretted.

Even now as she stood facing herself in the mirror with a glass of iced tea in one hand and a bottle of pills in the other, she didn't regret her decision. Tears streamed down her face as she swallowed handfuls of the small white pills. She cried out to God in the pain and loneliness of that moment as she attempted to end her life.

"Oh, God, I'm so tired! Please give me rest. Just let me go to sleep and not wake up! I just need to go to sleep," she sobbed.

How had it come to this?

No one else knew of the turmoil in her heart. She hadn't told anyone. She didn't want them to think that she wasn't perfect, that she couldn't handle things, that her life was out of her control. Maybe in ending her life she would gain some control.

Her thoughts raced back over the summer. She had graduated high school—barely missing honors, she reminded herself. If she hadn't graduated with honors, at least she could comfort herself with the fact that she almost had. "If it hadn't been for that German class and algebra!"

She had graduated on Friday. On Monday, she started work at a factory in the cookie department. She had worked long, hot days on those cookie belts. Often, they would call her to work at night too. She'd been told that you weren't supposed to turn them down. So she had worked whatever hours they asked her to. She hadn't really fit in with the ladies there. They didn't like the summer college help anyway. After work, they'd go to a local bar for drinks. She'd head home.

This summer she had had a boyfriend too. In her heart, she knew that he wasn't someone God wanted her with. He was involved in things that he shouldn't have been. He was pushing her to move their relationship into a physically intimate one. She kept saying No, but this past weekend, when he threatened to break up with her again, he'd said that next weekend they'd . . .

She knew that she needed out of the relationship, but she felt trapped. When she was home and didn't go along with him, he'd threaten to break up with her. While she was at school, she received notes from him, telling her that if she didn't come home each weekend or ever broke up with him, that they'd be burying his body in "a white, pine box." She wanted to end it, but how? Besides, at least she had a boyfriend, she reasoned.

This summer, she and several of her friends had been baptized at the Baptist church they attended. They'd been going there for years. Now that they were all graduating and heading in different directions, they'd decided to be baptized. She thought of Laurie. Laurie had a peace that filled her eyes. She wanted that peace but just couldn't seem to get it, no matter what she did.

Now here she was at college. She didn't really want to be here, not yet. Not until she figured out what she really wanted to do with her life. Yeah, she had selected a major—a double major. She always had been ambitious. And she had even listed a job goal that she was working for. *Human and public relations.* It sounded good. And she had heard it paid well. She thought it'd be fun having an office and dressing up, carrying a briefcase and working with people. But in the back of her mind, there was this question:

Is this what God wants for me? What does God want with my life?

She had never really asked Him. She had asked Him to be her Saviour but never the Lord of her life. And now everything was happening so fast. And people expected so much. And she tried so hard to please people.

If everything could just stop for a minute! Just long enough for me to think. To pray. To figure out what God wants. And how to get that peace.

But life didn't stop. It kept rushing past. Sweeping her up in it.

She wasn't helping it to slow down. She just kept doing more. Already she had joined the orchestra, had become a "soccer header," was working part time and going out for cheerleading. *If I can become a cheerleader, then I'll be someone. Maybe then I'll have that peace,* she thought.

But nothing helped. So here she stood. Swallowing handfuls of pills in a last ditch attempt to gain some control. Even if it would be the last control she would ever have.

God had other plans. As she lay down to sleep that night, crying, wondering if she would ever wake up again, He was with her.

He protected that young girl through the night and the next day. He cleared her head enough the next afternoon so that she could call Poison Control. They told her that if she was OK by then, she'd be fine and suggested she call Crisis Intervention. That was a long call. She had poured out her heart to the unknown person at the other end of the phone line. They had listened and encouraged her to tell someone what she had done.

Feeling better, she washed her face and went to the room of a friend. She told her friend about the pills. Then she went back to bed.

The friend told the floor monitor, who contacted the dorm mom. Together they got her now rag-doll-like body dressed and to the hospital. Her parents were called and came to see her. Her Sunday School teachers called and made plans to come visit. Her boyfriend called. She seemed fine. She'd be headed back to college by the end of the week.

Then her heart almost stopped and the peaceful sleep that she had so desired threatened to take her. "Don't go back to sleep," the nurse kept telling her. But the sleep felt so good. Peaceful. She wouldn't understand for several years how close she had come to dying that afternoon.

But she didn't die. She lived. She didn't go back to college. She went home to sort things out. She'd told her parents that she needed time to think. The counselor at the college suggested that she take a year off and come back the following fall. Somehow she knew she wouldn't. But for now, the door was still open. And she had time to think.

And so began my journey in learning to live like His daughter. I was that young-girl; trying to please, to measure up, to somehow be good enough. I couldn't see any value in myself. I kept thinking, *If only I did this or that, then I'll be somebody*. I felt like a nobody. And no matter how other people saw me, I just couldn't see myself as anything but hopeless.

But I was God's daughter. I had asked Him into my heart as a young child, claiming His eternal life and His grace. I had prayed to Him, and in my own feeble attempts had attempted to grow in Him. Finally, about six months after my suicide attempt, I finally surrendered all to Him, asking Him to take over my life. Asking Him to not only be my Saviour but the Lord of my life too. I finally admitted that I just couldn't do it on my own. All my attempts fell through. I was making a mess of things.

I'll never forget that afternoon. Kneeling by a log in the woods. Crying. Praying. Almost yelling. I poured out all my pain—my feelings of helplessness, of worthlessness, of hopelessness. How I longed to be somebody! I cried and sobbed till there was nothing left. I was honest before God, maybe for the first time in my young life. And God was big enough to take it. A peace filled me, and I felt the promise my pastor had shared with me earlier that day, *"His left hand is under my head, and His right hand embraces me"* (Song of Solomon 2:6).

God was holding me in His arms. He loved me. Still. After everything. I sat there in the woods for a while. Peaceful.

A different young woman came out of the woods that day. One who was intent on learning about God. Who was He? What did she believe? What did the Bible say? Where did she belong? What did God want from her?

A new journey began.

Reflection

1. Has there been a time in your life when you've asked Jesus to be your Saviour? If yes, why did you? What brought you to that place in your life? If you haven't, God may be leading you to make that commitment right now. Pray and ask Him in. *Heavenly Father, I know that I'm a sinner. I believe that Jesus died on the cross for me. Please come into my heart and life and be my Saviour. I claim the gift of eternal life and thank You for loving me. Help me to live like Your daughter. In Jesus' name, amen.*

2. Do you allow God to be Lord of your life? Looking to Him for direction? What is the difference between Saviour and Lord?

3. To you, what does it mean to "be somebody"? What do you do to try to "be somebody"? Does it work?

Prayer

O Lord, Adonai, help me to allow You to not only be my Saviour but to be the Lord of my life too. Show me what You want in my life. Help me to see that I am somebody in You—that I'm Your daughter. Show me how to live like Your daughter. In Jesus' name, amen.

two

What Will People Think?

When I entered the woods that day, I was searching for peace and for hope. For an end to my struggle to prove myself and to feel as if I belonged. I had been trying for so long to live up to an image that I thought people saw me as: someone who had it all together, whom others turned to for help, who was always willing to help out.

My people-pleasing was my attempt to earn love, to earn value. If others thought highly of me, I reasoned, then I might be valuable. When people criticized me, I felt as if I had failed. I didn't take their criticisms constructively, but destructively. I allowed the devil to use every criticism to affirm my worthlessness. It proved that I was nobody, that I'd never be anyone. I was hopeless.

Tracy has trouble handling criticisms too. She can't deal with people telling her what to do or how to do it. "Sometimes people are only making a suggestion, and I go off the deep end—sometimes verbally and sometimes just inside my own head," she shares. "The other day, my mom came over for a visit. I thought

I'd fix us some lunch, maybe a salad. As I was chopping onions, Mom asked, 'Why are you doing it that way? Why not use that chopper your father and I gave you?' Immediately I got defensive. It was my house, my kitchen. Why was she telling me how I should be doing something? I didn't say a word, but I fumed for the rest of the visit. Later I realized that maybe Mom just wanted to know that I liked the gift they gave me. She wasn't really telling me I was doing it wrong—like I thought."

Annette understands how Tracy feels. "I was working on a project at work. I had a deadline to meet, and the going was slow. I have to admit that I don't know a lot about our new computer program and all it's capable of doing. But when the new intern suggested I try laying out the presentation using something new, I felt threatened. I thought he felt he knew more than I did and that he could do a better job. I didn't thank him for his input and basically told him to mind his own business. It took forever to finish the project. He probably does know how to make the computer do what he wants. I could've used his help and maybe learned a few things for the future."

One weekend I came home from a women's retreat to find that Tim had moved the refrigerator and stove into the middle of the floor. He was cleaning the floor where they usually sit. "What are you doing?" I asked, as I tried kissing him Hello. "Thought I'd help you by cleaning under these." Immediately my defensive mechanism was triggered. *Does he expect me to move the appliances out and clean under them every week? I can't even budge them far enough to do that. I thought I was doing a pretty good job remembering to clean the top of the fridge.* I immediately assumed that he didn't think I cleaned well enough, that I should move the stove and fridge and clean under them. That wasn't what he was trying to say. He was trying to be helpful, to show me that he loved me by doing something he thought I might appreciate. Needless to say, I didn't wholeheartedly appreciate his help.

Wanting people to think well of us isn't wrong. It's when we base our value on what others think of us that we get into trouble.

Joyce learned at an early age that the way to gain her parents' approval was to please them. When she got good grades or did well in a school production, her parents were warm and encouraging. Her parents would brag about her grades and accomplishments. But if a grade didn't measure up, and during the times between accomplishments, her parents were silent. No encouraging words, no hugs. Joyce learned that to be loved, she needed to accomplish, to *earn* it. Her value became wrapped up in her accomplishments. Yet no matter how long her list of accomplishments got, it was never enough. Her hunger for love was never satisfied.

Betty learned this lesson too. Not only does she attempt to keep a long list of accomplishments but she shares them with others whenever she can. "Today I cleaned out all the closets and took the things we didn't need to Goodwill. At work, my boss told me I'm next in line for the promotion. He really thinks I'm doing a great job. Next week, I'm leading the children's theater in their new production. The prop crew said they never saw anyone who could handle the kids like I do. . . ." On and on she goes, trying to appear important. She longs for someone to affirm that she is. Friends tend to shy away from Betty. They tire of her constant list of accomplishments. If only they realized what she really wanted was love.

Betty also finds that she can't relax around friends. She's constantly wondering what they're thinking of her, trying to talk about things that will impress them, worrying about how she's coming across. She wants so much for someone to tell her she's valued.

Marie has found her own way of getting people's encouragement. And it works most of the time. It goes like this: When someone gives her a compliment, she puts herself down so that they'll compliment her more. "Oh, Marie, that was a wonderful dinner!" Marie responds modestly, "Well, thank you. I'm not a good cook, you know." Then she waits for the typical response, "You're a *great* cook! You make the best lasagna! You go to so much trouble."

"Sometimes I put myself down just so I can get a compliment," Marie shares. "People will be talking about someone who's good at something and I'll say, 'I'm not good at anything.' Usually, one or two people will start sharing things I'm good at."

But the good feelings Marie gets from these "encouraging words" are temporary. So she's driven to do it over and over.

Jen doesn't seek people's approval through compliments, but she is incredibly sensitive to what people say and how they respond—or don't respond—to her. A few weeks ago, Jen passed Katie on campus between classes. "Hi, Katie! How are things going? Are you free for lunch today? We could meet at the deli." Her smile quickly faded as Katie rushed off with a short response, "Not today, Jen." "I kept thinking, what have I done? Did I upset her somehow? I couldn't think of what I had done. I was upset all day."

Later Jen found out that Katie had just learned from one of her professors that her term paper needed a lot of work. She was ground out because of that and all the work she was going to need to do in a short time. "Her attitude had nothing to do with me. I had never thought about that. I just assumed I had done something."

Emma finds herself saying "I'm sorry" a lot. Her boss will ask her a question about a project she's working on and immediately she's apologizing, "I'm sorry. It's not how you want it to be? I can change it." A co-worker will ask her about her upcoming time off, and she quickly says, "I'm sorry. Did you want that week? I can take a different week." Usually there's no need for Emma to apologize. But she lacks confidence in herself, her abilities, and her decisions. "I just feel like I can't do anything right, or at least not as well as someone else. And I don't want to upset anyone or make anyone mad." Her friends all like her a lot—she's an incredibly sensitive and caring young woman. "But she's gotta stop saying 'I'm sorry' for everything!" one friend says.

Carol spends a lot of time alone. Her children are grown and married. Her husband died several years ago. She'd like to get out with friends, but most evenings after work find her home alone. The ladies at work and at her church are friendly. There are even several in her neighborhood who seem nice. And Carol longs to get out and do things with them. Or just talk and visit with someone. But she's afraid of reaching out. "I don't want to bother anyone. They have their families and things to do. They don't have time to spend with me anyway." So she sits by herself, waiting for someone to call or stop by. Her insecurities and lack of confidence keep her from reaching out, possibly to someone who's also waiting for someone to care.

Our insecurities cause us to react in many different ways. Have you seen yourself in any of these stories, or possibly all of them? Each of us is created with a need to belong and to have value. Yet so many of us struggle with a feeling of not belonging, of having no value. And no matter how good we try to be, no matter how hard we seek the approval of others, we're left feeling empty. *Alone.*

That's how I felt when I entered the woods that warm spring afternoon. But when I left the woods, something had changed. Peace had begun to grow in my heart. So had hope and joy. I was a different person. The journey had only just begun, and I anticipated it with excitement.

What had happened? What caused the change in me?

First, I was honest with God. I told Him exactly how I was feeling. The hurts, the expectations, the hopelessness, the fears— *everything.* And it probably wasn't pretty. I had been holding things in for a long time.

And God was big enough to take it. He already knew all about it. He just waited for me to give it to Him so He could take care of it. I had held on to it, trying hard to fix it myself. Finally I had let go and admitted my helplessness, that I couldn't make myself a good person. I couldn't live up to all the expectations I had. I couldn't be perfect.

That was OK with God. See, He had known that all along too. He knew I wasn't perfect and that I couldn't make myself perfect or even just good. And He had already taken care of it for me. He had sent His Son Jesus to die for me. And now Jesus was living and interceding for me. Jesus and the Holy Spirit would make me perfect. (But it would be a lifelong task!) God had already promised in Philippians 1:6, "Being confident of this very thing, that *He* who has begun a good work in you will complete it until the day of Jesus Christ" (emphasis mine).

Second, I realized anew God's love for me. After pouring out my heart and begging God to work in my life, to give me some direction and hope, I sensed His love. It had been His love that had drawn me to Him in the first place. I had come to Him because He loved me just as I was. I didn't have to prove anything or do anything. He already loved me. "I have loved you with an everlasting love; I have drawn you with loving-kindness" (Jeremiah 31:3, NIV). But I had been trying so hard to earn love and value that I had forgotten that my Father's love was there all along. *Unconditionally.* That God loved me and wanted a relationship with me.

Dr. M. Lloyd Erickson shares a story in his book, *The Embrace of God,* which illustrates this:

Eighteen-year-old Beth belonged to a fairly normal and healthy family. In fact, observers saw Beth as an ideal daughter. She was on the academic honor roll. She never was in trouble with school officials. She was captain of the cheerleading squad. She had many friends.

Nothing was drastically wrong inside Beth's home either. It was just that Beth seemed to overvalue her privacy. She ignored her parents and three siblings. Attempts at conversation by family members were greeted with a curt one-word mumble.

Beth was busy. Besides attending high school, she worked at McDonald's most evenings. Her parents looked forward to those times when she would be home. But they were repeatedly disappointed when their cherished daughter immediately retreated to her room and locked the door. Beth would emerge for the evening meal. But she ate little and conversed less. Family members felt increasingly rejected by their daughter and sister.

One evening her father managed to speak with Beth alone. Through tears of pain, he once again told Beth how much the family loved her and how they were hurt by her continued withdrawal from them.

Beth responded, "What have I done? I've never been in trouble. I'm not on drugs, and I don't smoke or drink. I've kept the household rules. I'm not pregnant. I go to church. I've made good grades. All these things I've done for you and mom, and you're still not satisfied."

A period of silence ensued before her father found words. "Beth, you have done many good things. You know I am extremely proud of you and your accomplishments. But I must comment on something you said. If you did all these things for your mother and me, you did them for the wrong reason.

"We did teach you principles for living. But not for our benefit—for yours! It is you who will benefit from the choices you've made. Not us."

At this point her father poured out his pain. He told Beth that he didn't want merely good behavior. He wanted a relationship. He wanted his daughter to talk, to laugh, to cry, and to share with the family.

Through misty eyes, he concluded, "Beth, we don't want just good behavior. We want you."

And that's what God wanted for me. What He wants for each of us. Right now. Every day. He wants a relationship with us. It's not the good works He desires. He wants us to talk to Him, laugh with Him, cry on His shoulder and share everything that is a part of our lives with Him. He wants us. He'll accomplish the good works through us as a result of our relationship.

As I came out of the woods that afternoon, I was determined to know God. To have a relationship with Him that went past just the "I-should-read-the-Bible-and-pray-every-day" relationship. One where I could share from my heart everything and anything. I wanted to know Him and trust Him like never before. I asked Him to open up truth to me. To show me what He was all about. And boy, has He blessed!

As I've grown in my relationship with Him, my need for the approval of others has diminished. I'm finding my value in Him— not in what others think. Oh, I still stumble and fall into the old traps, but not as often. His love brings me security. Confidence.

As we grow secure in God's unbounded delight in us, our need for other's approval will fade away. We'll no longer be tempted to boast of our accomplishments to impress people. We won't need to embellish a story to make ourselves look good. We'll stop seeking the ego boost that comes from being the center of attention. As our hearts are transformed by God's love, we will gradually become more consumed with helping others experience that love than trying desperately to get others to love us" (*Discipleship Journal*, July/August 1996, 43).

When we learn to trust Him totally—which can only happen as we grow in our relationship with Him—we will be able to trust Him with our reputations, with what others think, with our value and importance. And then we will be able to reach out to others with His love.

Our insecurities can cause us to be so focused on ourselves— our failures, our hopelessness, our lack of value—that we miss out on God's love. We don't experience it the way we should, the way God desires us to.

He loves us. Always, completely, no matter what. And it's only in His love that we can find the confidence to live like His daughters instead of like slaves to our own feelings of inadequacy.

As I returned home that afternoon, I had a new focus. Instead of focusing on all my faults and trying to prove myself, I was focused on knowing God, on living in His love, on abiding in Him. There alone would be my Source of hope and confidence.

Reflection

1. Which of these do you struggle with:
   - Seeking approval of others
   - Wanting to be important
   - Putting yourself down
   - Not accepting compliments
   - Worrying about what others think of you
   - Being too sensitive
   - Taking things too personally
   - Often getting on the defensive
2. How do these affect your relationships with others? With God? How do you feel about yourself?

3. Are you willing to give these struggles over to God? After praying, list ideas to help face these struggles as they come. (i.e. when someone compliments me, I'll just say Thank you and nothing else, or when someone doesn't speak to me and I'm afraid I've done something to offend them, I'll think it through prayerfully, asking God to show me if I have done anything to offend them. If I have, I'll make amends. If I haven't, I'll assume it's not me and act as if I haven't done anything.)

4. What is your relationship with God like? Are you willing to commit to getting to know Him—*really* know Him through a *real* relationship with Him?

Prayer

My Creator, Elohim, sometimes my focus is so much on me and my faults. It affects how I react to people and how I serve You. Help me to turn these struggles over to You. Please change me. Give me the freedom to live as Your daughter, trusting You with what people think, with who I am, and with all that happens. Help me to learn to know You and to trust You completely. In Jesus' name, amen.

three

Mirror, Mirror

She was a successful, intelligent woman. A college professor. She had a great sense of humor and a love for life. But she felt there was one thing missing from making her life perfect, one thing that would open doors and relationships.

Beauty.

She had always longed to be pretty. But in her eyes, beauty had evaded her.

One day, her mother showed her a picture of a pretty little girl. She assumed it was a picture of her sister, "the pretty one." But she learned the picture was of her. She had been a pretty little girl! With this realization, she felt that maybe she could be pretty now too. So she began the process of eating right, exercising, losing weight, choosing attractive clothes. She had her hair done and learned to apply makeup.

And suddenly, she *was* pretty. People looked at her in a different way. Men wanted to take her out. She had everything she ever dreamed of.

Or did she?

She realized that being pretty involves *work*. Denying herself foods she loves. Getting up earlier to get that "just right look." And the people who now paid attention to her—they really weren't the kind of friends she wanted.

She learned that everything she really wanted, she already had. Including Mr. Right—someone who fell in love with her because of who she was, not how she looked. This realization brought her freedom—freedom to be herself. It didn't matter if she was pretty or not; her life was the way she wanted it.

Sound like a movie? It is. But her struggle is one many of us women face. The longing to be thin and beautiful. It bombards us everywhere. TV. Magazines. Advertisements. Diet books are top sellers. Almost every magazine has a "lose weight fast" article—promising thinness and beauty almost instantly. Diets. Exercise. All designed to make us trim.

And we hear the underlying message loud and clear. You've got to be thin and pretty to be valuable.

Young girls and women take the message to heart as they starve themselves or purge themselves after a binge. The desire to be thin becomes an obsession that leads to eating disorders like anorexia and bulimia.

Others resort to surgery. I recently read an article of an actress who found her value in the role she played on TV. In order to keep the role, she felt she needed to be thin, which led to her battle with bulimia. After the role ended, her self-esteem plummeted. In order to help her get a new role, she had breast implants put in. The implants eventually leaked, and now she suffers from a chronic illness. Each day she lives with pain.

I've battled with the desire to be thin and pretty too. I've never been overweight but have constantly worried over gaining a pound or two. Skipping meals after eating a high calorie snack. Checking the mirror often. Trying to eat right and exercise—not in an effort to be healthy but to be thin.

Several weeks ago, Tim paid me a big compliment. "You haven't been obsessed about how you look lately. What's happened? I'm glad you've finally realized that you look fine." He's told me all along that I look great. (He even thinks I'm pretty!)

I hadn't realized the change. But God had been changing me slowly. As I've constantly grown more focused on my relationship with Him, other things have faded from importance. My confidence comes from Him, not from my appearance.

Chuck Swindoll once said on his radio program that people who battle low self-esteem are often very caught up in how they look. How they look becomes a mirror of their value. But that's not how God looks at us. God says that our beauty should come from within, not from outward adornment. My mom often points out people who she thinks are beautiful—not because of how they look but because of who they are. "Sue is one of the prettiest women I know, but it's because of who she is. And Cecelia, she's one of the kindest people; I just love her sense of humor! It's who they are that make them so beautiful!" Now she's not saying that they aren't pretty outwardly but that their real beauty is something much deeper. She often reminds me that she knows a lot of "pretty" women who really aren't very pretty.

Yet our appearance still matters to us.

Gerri is very aware of how she looks when she's around other people. She knows she's overweight and that people treat her differently. Sometimes it makes her want to stay away from people—and thus she shies away from social gatherings. Other times it makes her angry, and she tells herself she doesn't care what they think—as she eats a bowl of ice cream to comfort herself.

Sue is aware of how she looks when she's around people too. But she's found that when she puts aside her self-consciousness and thinks about others, she forgets about worrying about what others think. "When I'm around other people, like in a social gathering, I look at the people around me and wonder what's on their hearts, what's happening in their lives. I pray that God can use me to touch them with His love. Pretty soon I've forgotten about my size and what others are thinking, and I just enjoy getting to know people, trying to get past the surface and really care about them."

Sue has learned to take the focus off herself and focus on loving others with God's love. Sue is one of the most beautiful people I know, someone I know I can trust when I need a friend. She's never so focused on herself or her own problems that she doesn't have time to listen or care. She's someone I enjoy spending time with. It's not always easy for her. She battles at times to get past her fears and the desire to be thinner. But she's trusting God with helping win the battle instead of doing it herself.

God can help us feel good about who we are—inside and out.

He's the One who created us. "For You have formed my inward parts; You have woven me in my mother's womb. . . . My frame was not hidden from You, when I was made in secret, and *skillfully* wrought in the lowest parts of the earth. Your eyes saw my substance, being yet unformed. And in Your book they all were written, the days fashioned for me, when as yet there were none of them" (Psalm 139: 13, 15-17 margin; emphasis mine).

He made each one of us to be who we are. He chose our hair color, the color of our eyes, our bone structure, whether we would have freckles or not, how light or dark our skin would be. He created us "skillfully" just the way He wanted us to be. Unique. His creations.

How do we learn to be comfortable with our appearance? How can we learn to be more focused on developing that inner beauty?

First, we need to realize that our value doesn't come from what we look like. God doesn't love us more or less if we're tall, short, thin, overweight, freckled, gray-haired, beautiful, average. He loves us because we're His. He delights in us. But we can only accept His value as we grow in our relationship with Him. As we get to know Him, our confidence in Him will replace our lack of confidence in ourselves. Appearance will matter less.

That doesn't mean we won't care about how we look or that we don't need to take care of our bodies. But the emphasis will be on what's best, what's the healthiest choice for you. Not on being thin or beautiful. As we age, our bodies will grow older. That's inevitable. We won't look the same in our thirties as we did when we were teenagers. Age and babies change things. My friend Mary says turning forty changes things. Gravity sets in. But we can learn to age gracefully, without fearing and hating every wrinkle, gray hair, or added pound.

Taking care of ourselves may also help us to feel better about how we look too.

Take an honest look at yourself. Don't compare yourself to anyone else. Is your weight good for your age and height? Are you taking care of yourself—getting enough sleep, drinking enough water, exercising a couple of times a week, eating a balanced diet? Are there emotional triggers that tempt you to eat things you shouldn't? Are you spending too much of your budget on clothes—trying to get that perfect look or keeping up with the latest trends? What are the things you don't like about how you look and why? Are they things you can do something about? Are you willing to put forth the effort to change? Why do you want to change? Here are some places to start:

Realistically assess your weight. Are you at a healthy weight? Then you need to maintain it. Are you overweight? Being overweight is unhealthy. Our bodies don't work well with the extra pounds. We need to take steps to lose that extra weight. Not because losing the weight will make us a better person but because it's good for us. It will make us healthier.

My mom is currently attempting to lose weight. Her doctor told her not to try to take it off all at once. Permanent weight loss occurs slowly. Half a pound a week is fine. The most important thing is to make lifestyle changes that you can live with every day for the rest of your life. If eating salad three times a day for the rest of your life is impossible for you (it would be for me), then don't try. Diets don't work. Learn to eat making right choices. Don't think of it as a diet, as something you will stop when you reach your desired goal. Plan eating habits that you will enjoy for the rest of your life. For most of us this means including things that are delicious but not healthy once in awhile. Don't *deny* yourself foods; just *choose* not to eat them right now. Telling yourself you *can't* have something makes most people want it even more.

Start walking with a friend. Or exercise in a way you enjoy. I love to walk. I love to walk even more when I'm walking and talking with a friend. I can put in more miles that way, plus I get to spend time with a friend. I also enjoy doing a few simple spot exercises while I'm watching TV. I'm not one to just sit doing nothing. Exercising while I'm watching the news takes care of two things at once. I don't enjoy the rowing machine Tim bought me the Christmas after I had Zachary. I'm sure he was trying to be thoughtful. He knew that I wanted to trim off the extra baby weight. The machine sits in a corner of the basement gathering dust. True, it would work and help me to firm up, but it's not exercise that I enjoy, so I'm not consistent at doing it. My friend Sue doesn't enjoy walking, but she loves her exercise machine and uses it most mornings before work. Exercise doesn't just help us to feel better physically. It helps us feel better emotionally and mentally too. It's worth trying to make room in your schedule for it—you'll never "find" the time.

Plan ahead. Decide what the emotional triggers are that send you to the corner store for half a gallon of ice cream. Decide now what you can do when they hit. I know that when I'm upset or feel hurt, I gravitate toward something sweet. Knowing this, I plan ahead what I'll do when I feel that way. Sometimes I call a friend. Or grab a glass of water. Often I just put off reaching for the sweet until after I've done something else. By then the craving is often gone. Try splurging on a bubble bath instead of that splurge on extra calories. Turn on some good music and sing along. Plan ahead when you're shopping. If it's not in your house, you'll be less likely to eat it. I try not to buy things I know will be too much of a temptation for me. I keep plenty of water and easy-to-grab munchies, like grapes and little carrots, on hand instead. (I often keep a bowl of grapes by the computer when I'm working. Writing is just frustrating enough to send me in search of something to munch on.)

Remind yourself of what's really important. I've had to keep reminding myself—over and over—that my goal is to be healthy, not to be a certain weight or size. Remember that your friends like you because of who you are, not because of your size or looks or clothes. And God loves you unconditionally.

Pamper yourself. There are a couple of things I do just for me to make me feel better about how I look. One is the basket of scented lotions and sprays on my dresser. For me, they're a treat. I can't wear perfumes because they give me a headache. These lotions and sprays are light. They keep my skin soft and smell great. One friend treats herself to pretty underthings—not just white but colorful ones. Things that make her feel feminine. When we had a bathtub (we only have a shower now), I would occasionally treat myself to a candlelight bubble bath. Locking myself in (it was the only time I had to myself) and playing soft music (it helped to drown out the kids at the door) was a little retreat.

As a child, a treat meant something sweet. Granny would bring candy bars or take us out for ice cream. That was special. When we want to treat ourselves, often we think of food. Learn to treat yourself to something else. A book or bubble bath. A call to a friend. We may need to learn to change our way of thinking. I try not to use the word "treat" for food with my boys. Our special times may include food—but aren't limited to it. A treat may mean a stop at the park to play tennis or basketball together. Or snuggling and reading a book together. As we learn to associate a treat with things we enjoy—not necessarily food—we may learn to do something other than reach for food when we want to pamper ourselves or make ourselves feel better. (And the boys would much prefer a "treat" of hiking in the mountains than eating a candy bar.)

Use the buddy system. Share your struggles and goals with a friend. Ask her to keep you accountable. My prayer partner will often ask what I'm doing for myself, or I'll ask if she's exercising and eating right. Make a promise to call each other when the battle gets especially tough. Share with them how you feel about yourself. Let them tell you what they see when they look at you. And *listen* to what they say. Have them write it down so you can remind yourself if you need to. Believe them. Their perspective of you will be different from yours. They see you through love.

Remember that how we look is only a part of who we are. When people see us, they see more than just how we look. They see our personality. Our sense of humor. Our caring. A smile can do a lot too.

Don't give up. If you eat a dozen cookies today, don't give up. Tomorrow is a new day. Lamentations reminds us that God's mercies are new every morning. Forgive yourself. Make a plan of how to handle the situation next time. Give it to God. He knows what you're struggling with. He knows what you need. Allow Him to win the battle for you.

I may or may not ever be beautiful in the eyes of others, but I can be content with who I am. Who I am is more than just what I look like. I can take care of myself, doing little things to make me feel better about myself. I can believe my husband when he says he thinks I'm pretty. I can exercise for at least a few minutes each day. Not only does that help how I look, but it helps me to feel better too. I can take control of my attitudes and eating, instead of letting them control me. And I can thank God that He's created me in His image. And recreating me into that image daily. He made each of us unique. Each of us is beautiful to Him. Freckles, gray hair, and all.

Reflection

1. Are your looks/weight overly important to you? Are they a big part of your thoughts a lot of the time? Do you feel as if people would like you better if you were thinner, prettier, etc.?
2. Realistically, make a list of the things you don't like about yourself.
3. Now, go back over the list. Which things *can* you change? Which are you *willing* to put forth effort into changing?
4. How can you change these things? Write down some realistic goals you could start today.
5. Make a list of the things you do like about whom God has created you to be. (At least five items!)
6. Think of someone who you think is pretty. What makes them pretty? Is it really their looks or more who they are?

Prayer

El Roi, You are the God who sees, You know how I feel about myself. The things I don't like, the things I do. Lord, as You see my lists and the goals I've set to change things, I give them to You. Please give me the peace to accept myself as You've made me and the strength and courage to change the things I should. Thank You for creating me in the way that You knew was best; creating me to be the me You wanted for Your daughter. Help me to see myself as more than just looks but as Your daughter, special to You, loved. Help me to be beautiful from the inside out. In Jesus' name, amen.

four

Baseball, Perfectionism, and Rainbows

I joined the church baseball team because I wanted to do something with other church members that would be fun, something besides working together. I also figured I needed the exercise.

I've always enjoyed playing baseball, but I'm not the greatest player. I can hit the ball when it's pitched to me, most of the time enough to get to first. And I can field a few grounders, though popups make me nervous. But I wasn't thinking about my shortcomings as much as I was thinking of the fun of being part of a team and playing.

Then the season started. There was some pressure on the women of the team. We were in a community league with a number of rules. One was that there had to be at least four women playing at all times. You could play five women and then have ten people playing, but you had to have four women. And only six women had signed up. Of course, everyone couldn't come to every game, so there was always the chance that we wouldn't have enough women and have to forfeit the game (although we never forfeited a game due to a lack of women!). Several of the men had the idea that the women couldn't really play. They were reluctant to throw to a woman, though our first and second bases were covered by women (I have to say that more of the men were encouraging than discouraging). But with this added pressure, we headed for our first game.

We lost. Big time. Twenty-something to something under ten. Plus one member of our team was hit in the face by a ball and required several stitches. I found that though I hit the ball, it usually popped up in the infield—an automatic out. I wasn't having fun.

See, I'm a perfectionist. I want to do everything perfectly. I don't want to let people down. I didn't want anyone to think I was a rotten player. I didn't like the fact that every time I was up to bat, I made an out. When we were in the field, I played right field, waiting for a ball to come that way, hoping that it wouldn't for fear that I'd miss it.

There was one game in particular where I did exceptionally bad. By this time in the season, I didn't enjoy going to the games, knowing I was going to fail, knowing I'd be the reason for a number of outs. I tried to get out of going but kept reminding myself that they needed me in order to have enough women. *Besides*, I kept telling myself, *I'm not playing just to win; I joined the team to have a good time.*

My first time up to bat I got a hit. Grounded it right to the player at first base. "Saves me from running," I joked as I returned to the bench. Once back out in right field, I prayed for angels to help me with the game. I talked to God through the next inning. (Right field can be a pretty lonely place when you're someone who enjoys talking!) But this time when I was up to bat, I struck out. I had never done that before. Tears threatened. *Don't cry, it's just a game, you're a grown up,* I kept telling myself. My oldest son, Joshua, tried encouraging me. He knew how I felt. Joshua had felt that way many times during the school year when he hadn't done well playing ball or on a test. Joshua inherited my perfectionist nature. I had told him all year that it didn't matter if he struck out or didn't get 100 percent on a test. That what counted was the effort he gave. Here was my opportunity to show him that I meant it.

Back in right field, I began praying again. Then I saw it. A rainbow. One of those kinds that circle the sun and you can just see a part of it on each side. *A rainbow! God's promise! You're promising to help me, aren't You? I'll do better my next up to bat!* Nervously I stepped up to the plate when it was my turn. I didn't swing at every ball. I chose carefully. Soon I had two strikes and three balls. *This is it,* I thought as the next ball was pitched.

"Strike three!"

The game never got better. Our team lost. I struck out every time I was at bat. Every time I was in the field, I prayed. I kept watching the rainbow. Wasn't it God's promise? Why was He letting me strike out?

Then His voice spoke softly to me in my frustration. *"The rainbow is a promise. A promise that I will love you no matter what. Even if you strike out."*

God's love for me—for you—is unconditional. He loves us even when we don't do things perfectly. Even when we strike out, mess up, or fall down. He sent His Son to die for us *while* we were still sinners. "But God demonstrates His own love toward us, in that while we were still sinners, Christ died for us" (Romans 5:8). He doesn't wait for us to become perfect. He loves us right now, no matter what. He already knows all about us, even our worst sins. He knows that we will strike out, mess up, and fall down. But He offers us hope and help each time.

So why do we think we have to be perfect? Why are we so afraid to let others see us fail, to share our struggles and fears?

We know that everyone isn't perfect. We know that we each fail and make mistakes. And when we learn of another's struggle or fault, we attempt to encourage them, pray for them, love them anyway. Yet we hesitate to let others do the same for us.

When we don't allow anyone to see us fail or to share a

struggle or fear, we miss out on the encouragement and prayers of others.

We also miss out on making ourselves vulnerable and giving others the opportunity of saying "Hey, I feel like that sometimes too!" or "I've struggled with that." Sharing our own struggles and mistakes opens the door for others to share with us, to talk to us, to come to us for advice.

When I shared the story of my suicide attempt with a young woman going through a similar experience, it opened the door for her to talk to me. She realized that I understood some of what she was going through. It also gave her parents hope that it wasn't the end of the world. I had lived through that time of my life, and God was doing incredible things in my life. It gave them hope that He would do the same for their daughter. If I had never shared my experience, they may have faced this struggle in their lives feeling very alone.

It doesn't mean that we're going to share every mistake, fault, and struggle with everyone we meet. There are times and places to share. But we have to be willing to admit that we're not perfect. We can't always handle everything.

Tracy was feeling pretty alone. She had received devastating news from home. She was close to tears all weekend. "My friends are going to think I'm crazy soon," she half joked, "because I keep bursting out into tears." But she was unwilling to share her struggle. "I should be able to handle this on my own. What would other people think?"

A teacher felt impressed to talk to Tracy, not knowing what was happening in her life. Finally Tracy confided everything, crying, trying to appear in control. "Why do you think you have to be perfect, Tracy?" she asked. "Don't you think other people already know that you're not? Don't you think your friends would love to help you through this? To pray with you, encourage you? Don't you enjoy being there for your friends? Why not let them be there for you? You

don't have to share everything with them. Just tell them you're struggling; ask them to pray. Let them carry you. God didn't mean for us
to do it alone. He created us in families. He created Eve for Adam,
saying it wasn't good for people to be alone. He gave us church
families and friends and told us to encourage one another. Why not
let people? You can't do that if you're trying to make everyone think
you're perfect."

Tracy thought about her words. The teacher was right. But it
was hard. She had always been the one everyone else had come
to for help. She didn't want people to think less of her. But people
often think more of us as we admit our faults and struggles. It
draws them to us as we trust them enough to share with them.
It's easier to be friends with someone who isn't perfect—when
you know you're not perfect yourself—than to be friends with
someone who's perfect. Someone who always does everything
right, whose home is always spotless, whose kids always behave,
who always looks wonderful. It's hard to be around someone like
that, because it's a constant reminder that you don't live up.

Tracy knew, too, that her friends looked up to her. Admitting that she struggled, too, would help her friends not see her as
someone they could never live up to but as a person just like
them who struggled, failed, succeeded, cried, and rejoiced.

Sometimes when we think we have to do everything perfectly, it causes us not to try new things because we're afraid we
won't be able to do them right. My grandfather always told my
mom that she could go swimming once she knew how. But how
was she ever going to learn to swim if she didn't try?

There have been many things I haven't attempted for fear I
wouldn't be able to do them perfectly the first time. Or for fear I
might look silly in front of others, or not be able to do them as
well as they could.

Like water-skiing. Tim and his friends water-skied every weekend during the summer for a year or two. They invited me to go

along and try it. But I always found an excuse why I couldn't. Once in a while I would go to the lake and even ride in the boat, but I wouldn't try to ski because I was afraid I wouldn't be able to get up. They could all ski wonderfully. They used trick skis and slalom skis. Even my son tried. But I wouldn't.

Then one summer, they coaxed me into trying it on an empty lake. No one was around. I determined that I'd try. Tim enjoyed it so much. I didn't want to be left sitting on the shore all the time. Getting up was hard. I finally did it. For thirty wonderful seconds, I was skimming across the top of the lake! It was exciting! I kept thinking of Peter and how incredible it must've been to walk on water. Then I fell. Tim encouraged me not to try anymore for then, so that my muscles wouldn't be too sore the next day. After that, I couldn't wait to try again. But they never went water-skiing again. All the chances I had, I had passed up. Now I no longer have the opportunity.

Carin was afraid to try downhill skiing. Her husband often went with several friends. And she'd gone along a few times. But she didn't like flying down icy hills at breakneck speed out-of-control. She was constantly afraid that she would fall down. She knew others fell. Her husband and his friend Lance seem to even enjoy falling down. But Carin wanted to do it perfectly. For her, that meant never falling or failing.

It also meant that she was missing out on something fun with her husband.

Is not doing something until we can do it perfectly worth missing out on all the fun things we could be trying and doing now? Is it worth trying something and failing and possibly enjoying yourself anyway, even if you look silly? And maybe you won't look silly. Maybe you'll be able to do it great or love it—but you won't know until you try. And maybe looking silly will be more fun that doing it perfectly!

When I came home discouraged after the ballgame that I had struck out at, I shared with Tim my feelings of failure and inadequacy. "I'm just not good at baseball. I struck out three times and grounded my only hit right to the player at first base," I whined.

"You know, Babe Ruth had the most home runs of anyone in his time," responded my wise husband, "but he also had the most strikeouts."

Babe Ruth could never have had the record home runs if he hadn't risked striking out. Am I willing to risk a few strikes to someday get a home run?

I've learned that sometimes God's version of perfect and mine are different. For me, perfect may mean never failing or messing up—always saying the right words, doing the right things. When I would go to speak to groups of ladies, I would pray and pray beforehand that God would bless, that I would share His words and not mine. Then all the way home, I would beat myself up over what I had said, how the meeting had gone. Why did I say that? I forgot to share this. Then one day, God spoke to me gently as I beat myself up, "Tami, didn't you pray about this? Didn't you ask Me to make it go the way I wanted it to? Did you ask Me for the right words?"

"Well, yes."

"Then are you willing to trust that no matter how you feel, I accomplished what I wanted? That everything went just the way I planned?"

Trusting God with the results and how things went brought me real freedom. I didn't have to beat myself up over everything that didn't go the way I wanted. I could trust that He had answered my prayer and accomplished what He desired.

I didn't have to be perfect. I just had to allow Him to work and then trust Him.

Sometimes we have to risk failing, risk not being able to do things perfectly, risk not looking perfect in order to learn, to be open to others who are struggling, to enjoy life. We have to learn to trust God as we give Him each part of our life and day.

I was listening to Chuck Swindoll on the radio one afternoon, and he shared a story from his early ministry. Each morning when he arrived at his office, a friend would call him.

"Hello?" Chuck would answer.

"Hello, Chuck, this is God calling. I just want to give you permission to fail today." Click. Chuck would sit and smile at the empty receiver. Permission to fail, to mess up, to struggle.

God gives each of us permission to fail. He offers His forgiveness when we sin, His wisdom when we need to learn, His peace when we just can't be perfect, and His love no matter what.

Are you willing to risk not being perfect today?

Reflection

1. Do you struggle with looking perfect? What does it mean to you to "be perfect"?
2. Are there things you've put off because you weren't sure you could do them perfectly? If Yes, what are they, and what were you afraid of? What would be the worse thing that could happen if you tried and what you feared most happened? How bad would that be?
3. Are you willing to give yourself permission to fail? Are you willing to honestly share your struggles with others? What would the advantages be? The disadvantages?

Prayer

Dear heavenly Father, thank You for not waiting till I was perfect to love me, for loving me unconditionally right now. Help me to accept Your unconditional love and allow myself to try and to fail and to share with others my struggles—not to always have to look perfect to others. And as I share, help me to minister to others who are struggling too. In Jesus' name, amen.

five

The Words We Hear

She was sweating profusely. "Ninety-eight, ninety-nine, one hundred," she whispered, out of breath. "I just did one hundred deep knee bends." But her satisfaction was short-lived.

"Do you think that makes you look like Cindy Crawford? Do you know how much she weighs?"

"I'd hate to guess."

"And she's five feet taller than you."

Kathy accepted the inner rebuke and decided to do her push-ups. She had been working on strengthening her arms for weeks, and she could now do five push-ups in a row. She was finished with her warm-ups and was ready for her morning walk.

She was stretching her calf muscles by pushing against the garage door frame. Since the door was up, she stared inside, appalled at the accumulation of years.

"If you were any kind of housekeeper, you'd put that stuff where it belongs."

"But it doesn't belong anywhere. Most of it is junk."

"Then why haven't you sorted through it and given it to the homeless shelter?"

"I'll think about it when I get back."

Kathy had a fairly peaceful walk. She usually walked about a mile. She had been trying hard to get in shape. Having put on a few extra pounds over the last few years, she desperately wanted to shed them. She was only a block from the house when the Coach spoke again.

"You're so fat! How could you let yourself get this way?"

Kathy tried to ignore the voice the best she could (Paul & Nicole Johnson, *Random Acts of Grace*, 110, 111).

Kathy continues through her day in this story titled "The Coach." Yet throughout her day, she hears the voice of the "Coach." A voice that constantly criticizes, critiques, and corrects her. The voice tells her that she doesn't take great care of her family, that she's not doing enough to witness to her neighbors, that she's not active enough in church, nor is she doing enough things in her relationship with Christ. Sure, she reads her Bible and prays, but she's not memorizing scripture. Yes, she's involved in many things in church, but she's not on the prayer chain. Constantly throughout her day, this voice reminds her that she's just not good enough.

What do the voices you listen to tell you about you?

Katie enjoys staying home with her children. She plants a garden each spring and spends the end of summer and early fall months canning and freezing. She bakes her own bread and sews her daughter's clothes. She keeps her home neat and clean. But she never feels like it's enough. She's sure there's more that she should be doing. The voices in her head are from her past. "You're lazy. Look at this room! You'll never amount to anything. I'll have to bring a shovel to get through your house when I come to visit."

Kimberly is an associate in a law firm. She has a solid client base and is respected by those in her office. She has a reputation for being fair and honest, hard-working. But she constantly pushes herself. Constantly trying to learn more, do better, be more efficient. She keeps remembering the words of a junior high school teacher, "You've got to try harder. You're not living up to your potential. You could do so much more, Kim."

Sometimes the words we hear are from our past. They are words spoken by parents and teachers and our peers. Words that replay themselves in our minds, telling us we can't do something, that we're lazy or stupid. Words that constantly remind us that we're not good enough.

They may be words from society. Words that tell us we need to look a certain way or hold a certain job or degree. The world tells us that to be someone special we have to do something spectacular, be a superstar. So we keep on pushing, striving to be the best. Maybe they're words from church; causing us to feel like we have to serve more, do more, or be perfect.

And we believe these words. We listen to them over and over in our heads. They affect what we do and how we feel about ourselves. Sometimes we spend much of our energy trying to prove the words wrong. We try harder, take on more projects, become compulsive about how we look or what we eat. All in an effort to please someone or prove ourselves to someone so that they'll tell us we're OK.

Too often we look for confirmation of who we are in those around us. We wait for others to tell us that we're someone, that we're special. Yet God has said it all along.

"I have loved you with an everlasting love; therefore with lovingkindness I have drawn you" (Jeremiah 31:3).

"I have called you by your name, you are Mine . . . you were precious in My sight, you have been honored, and I have loved you" (Isaiah 43:1, 4).

The Bible tells us that God delights in us (Isaiah 62:4) and that He created us just for Him (Isaiah 43:21). He has chosen us and made us His special treasure (Psalm 135:4). His Word is full of reminders of His love; reminders that we are His. We are His children, His treasure, His special possession, His beloved. But we don't listen to His words.

Henri Nouwen writes in *Life of the Beloved*:

> Though the experience of being the Beloved has never been completely absent from my life, I never claimed it as my core truth. I kept running around it in large or small circles, always looking for someone or something able to convince me of my Belovedness. It was as if I kept refusing to hear the voice that speaks from the very depth of my being and says: "You are my Beloved, on you my favor rests." That voice has always been there, but it seems that I was much more eager to listen to other, louder voices saying: "prove that you are worth something; do something relevant, spectacular or powerful, and then you will earn the love you so desire." Meanwhile, the soft, gentle voice that speaks in the silence and solitude of my heart remained unheard or, at least, unconvincing.

We tell ourselves that Jesus loves us. That God loves us so much that He sent His only Son to suffer and die for us. We talk about how He's given each of us talents and abilities. How He's created each of us unique and special—with the personality and talents which He wanted us to have. We say that we believe we can't earn salvation. That we can't do anything to make God love us more or to be more His. But do we *really* believe? Do we really accept His Word deep in our hearts? Does it make a difference in how we feel about ourselves? Or are we still listening to the voices around us and feeling hopeless . . . unworthy . . .

lazy . . . useless . . . untalented . . . not special. Are we still trying to prove ourselves, trying to do something to make someone love us, accept us, desiring so much to be loved and accepted but never feeling it or believing it?

Yet God does love us and accept us. Just as we are.

We're kind of like the ugly duckling. Remember the story? A mother duck hatches a nestful of eggs. And one of the ducklings doesn't look like the rest. He's bigger and awkward and in the eyes of those in the barnyard, ugly. The other ducklings tease him and make fun of him—constantly telling him how ugly he is. And he believes them. Crushed and discouraged, he runs away from the barnyard. He sees no value in himself. Till one day he sees his reflection in the water and realizes that he's not a duckling but a swan. A beautiful, graceful swan. Of course, he was a swan all along. But he chose to believe the words of those around him. Chose to believe that he was ugly and worthless. He let it affect how he acted and felt about himself. Yet that day, when he realized he was a swan, he was able to let go of all those past words. He was a swan, a beautiful swan. He could slide gracefully across the pond. He held his head up high. There was no reason to be ashamed any longer.

And we have no reason to be ashamed of who we are. We are God's swans, not ugly ducklings. We need to see our reflection in the light of His Word and believe—really believe. We must believe that we are His daughters, that we are loved and accepted. Right now, just as we are. And live like we believe His Word, like we believe we are loved and accepted.

It's hard to let go of past words, to stop hearing the voices in our heads. Those voices are all around us each day, telling us what we should be and what we aren't. But God can free us of them.

The place to begin is by filling our minds with God's Word. Reading His Word, searching His Word, looking for how He feels about us. Underline them, maybe all in one color—like purple, the color of royalty (we are princesses, aren't we?) so that they're easily found. Memorize them. Write them on 3 x 5 cards and carry them with you, memorizing them throughout the day, while you're waiting in traffic or in line at the store or for an appointment. Write verses on Post-its and stick them to the bathroom mirror or above your kitchen sink or desk. Put them someplace where you will see them and be reminded of God's love. That in God's eyes, you have nothing to prove, nothing to live up to, nothing to live down. You're forgiven. You're loved with an everlasting love. You're His treasure. Part of His jewels (Malachi 3:17).

You may want to look up specific verses to counter the words you hear, verses that you can tell yourself when you hear the old voices. If you constantly are reminded of past sins, look for verses that tell of God's forgiveness. If you feel worthless, look for verses that tell you how precious you are to the Father. If you feel hopeless, look for verses of hope.

Sometimes the words we hear may be true. We have to accept that and let it drive us closer to Jesus. As I sit here writing this, I'm overwhelmed with my own inadequacies. *Why am I doing this? What do I have to share? Can what I've learned help anyone else? I'm not trained or educated . . . who am I to be doing this?* I know me. I am inadequate on my own. My faults and problems loom large in my mind. And I'm tempted to quit. To not try. To give up and give in to these feelings. But instead, I run to God. *Lord, I am inadequate. And You know my faults and struggles. But Lord, You've taught me so much. I want to share the freedom and confidence You've brought me. Polish my words. Speak through me. Fill in my inadequacies. Let Your love and Spirit flow through me.* Instead of letting my inadequacies keep me from writing, I use these feelings and knowledge to drive me closer to Him, to cause me to lean on Him for the words and ideas. And He is faithful. He can take my inadequacies, my weaknesses, and add His gifts to make what He desires. I trust Him to do that. It's what keeps me going. If the words you hear are true, let them drive you to depend on Jesus to change you, to work through you, instead of allowing them to discourage you or make you feel worthless. Remember, in our weakness, He is strong.

Realize where the voices are coming from. *From the devil.* He wants to constantly discourage you, to cause each of us to feel hopeless, worthless. He likes it when we're so busy trying to prove ourselves and make people like us that we don't see the needs and pain in the lives of others. He doesn't want us to experience the joy and freedom that God gives. Joy in trusting God with everything. Freedom in being ourselves and growing—slowly as we get to know our Father better. Trusting God—not ourselves—to complete the work in us. We can never make ourselves good enough or make others like us. We will never be able to achieve enough. But that's OK. All God asks of us is that we be His, that we be faithful and trust Him.

In the story of Kathy and her "Coach," Kathy cries out to God asking what she has to do to be good enough. She's tried doing all the Coach tells her she has to, but she's tired. Tired of trying, of pushing, of never being good enough, of the voices. And then the voice is silent. And in the silence, she hears a quiet voice.

Then a voice came, but it wasn't the Coach. *"Why do you hate yourself?"* It was a small voice, and so gentle it made Kathy cry harder.

"I don't know; I just do. It feels like I can never do enough."

"For whom?" the gentle voice asked.

"For anybody, for everybody, I don't know. I just try so hard, and I never seem to get anywhere."

"Where do you want to get?"

Kathy realized it the moment He asked it. "I want everyone to like me." Her tears spilled down her cheeks. "But that won't ever happen, will it?"

She did not need an answer. Not only did she know it would never happen, but if it did happen, it still wouldn't be enough. "My needs are so huge," she confessed honestly. "I want everyone to notice what I do and love me for it. Then I hate them for making me perform."

At that moment, Kathy had a revelation. "My husband, my mother, my pastor, and all my friends could love and accept me, but I would still want more...." She paused, putting the pieces together. "Because I don't accept me. And I know that if there is one person on this planet who doesn't love me, then I will side with that person, because that's how I feel about myself."

"Can I tell you how I feel about you?" the tender voice spoke again.

"Yes," she whispered through her tears. "Yes, please" (*Random Acts of Grace*, 118, 119).

Whose voice are you listening to?

Choose to listen to what God says about you. He knows you best.

Reflection

1. What are the words you hear most often? Do they discourage you or drive you closer to God? How can you cause them to drive you closer to Christ?
2. What does the Bible say about how God sees you? What are His words about you?
3. How can you choose to listen to God's words? What will you choose to do today?

Prayer _____

    Abba, Father, you know the words I listen to each day. They cause me to feel discouraged. They make me try harder, to constantly strive to be something, someone. Help me to rest in who You say I am. Help me to search for and listen to the words You say. Imprint them on my mind. Help me to live as if I believe what You say. Thank You for Your love. Thank You for loving me just as I am. I love You, Father. In Jesus' name, amen.

six

Learning to Say No

My friend Daniel can say "No!" In fact, Daniel's mom thinks he says it all the time.

"Daniel," she patiently asks. "Please pick up your toys."

"No."

"Daniel, it's time for bed."

"No."

"Daniel, be nice to the doggie."

"No."

"Daniel, share your toy with Courtney."

"No."

Daniel is two years old. The word *no* is new for him. It gives him control, a choice. Like many two-year-olds, he can say it well. But somewhere along the line, we forget how to say No. We end up saying Yes to too many things. Why?

Somewhere along the way, I got the idea that the more I did, the more people would like me. The more value I'd have.

I didn't want to let anyone down. Or have anyone think I couldn't do it all.

Doing some things gave me a sense of importance. A title. A position.

I kept looking for something that would make me feel important—valuable.

But the more I was willing to do, the more people asked me to do things. It got to a place where if no one else was willing to do something, I was asked. Everyone knew I wouldn't say No. At least that's how it felt to me.

Most of my time was spent doing something for someone. Most of the time, it was all good things. Important things. Things that had to be done by someone.

But the problem was that I was running out of time. I couldn't do everything—though I wasn't admitting that yet. I still struggled to get everything done. Plus, I had a home to take care of, a husband, two sons, family, friends, and a God who all wanted some of my time too. Something had to give.

When I looked at all I was doing, it was hard to decide what had to go. It was all so important or meant so much to me. But I found that I didn't have time to spend with God. Tim was getting an exhausted wife at the end of the day. I didn't have time to play with the boys and was often short with them. It wasn't fair to them. One day we spent the entire day at church. From 9:00 a.m. (Tim and Joshua were choristers, and I was a greeter) till after nine o'clock that evening (there was a social). There was potluck and a meeting, and then something wasn't working right with the new satellite equipment, and there was something that needed taping that afternoon. So Tim tried figuring out what was happening while I visited and prayed with a friend whose husband had left her there while he went with the pastor to take Communion to shut-ins. The boys played nicely and read books from the library. But by evening, they had had it. Along with several other children, they spent a portion of the church social destroying a SS classroom. Beanbag frogs were strewn everywhere with beans all over the floor. Felts were here and there. Stuffed animals lay scattered throughout the mess. That was when I realized how wrong it was of me to ask the boys to sit through so much in one day. I realized that my schedule had to change. I said that God was my top priority and that Tim and the boys were next, but my schedule didn't reflect it. I was constantly doing something, running here and there. Time with God was sporadic. Time as a family was nonexistent. It was time for a change.

But how do we change? How do we learn what to say Yes to and what to say No to?

1. Don't answer right away. When someone asks you to do something, ask for time to pray about it or to check your calendar. Sometimes I tell them that I need to talk to Tim. (Talking to Tim often causes me to have to say No, but it also keeps me from overscheduling.) I read the story of one lady who was very busy doing good things. Then she was told that she had cancer and had only a short time to live. Time became very important to her. It no longer was just something to spend but to use carefully. She stopped saying Yes to everything. Instead, she asked for time to pray about it. At first, she did this with only big things. but soon began to ask for time to pray or to check her calendar even for simple things, like spending time with a friend. Sometimes our lives can be eaten up with lots of small commitments that keep us rushing here and there. Asking for time first gave her a chance to see if it was something God wanted her to do. It changed her life and helped her keep her priorities. Later she found that she didn't have cancer, but she had learned an important lesson that she didn't forget.

2. Pray about it, no matter how big or simple it is. Ask for God's leading. God will never give us more to do than we can. He never wants us to feel burdened or rushed or overwhelmed. One of my perpetual calendars says "Never take on more than you have time to pray about." I'd like to add, "If you don't have time to pray about it, don't take it on."

At this point you may be thinking, but if I say No, who will do it?

If God wants it done, He'll get it done.

If He wants it done, He has someone to do it. And if it's not you, it's someone else. If you take on something that God doesn't want you to, you may be preventing the person He has in mind from doing what God desires.

And it's possible that God may not want it done. At least not for now. But we need to learn to be obedient and trust God.

But what if the person doesn't do it "right"? Can I trust God with that?

I've struggled with all these. Our nominating committee has been meeting to decide who should serve in what capacity for the coming year. For six years, I've been leading the local Women's Ministries program. I started the program, and it's important to me. I love the ladies in my church and have enjoyed planning fun things for them and programs that will help them grow spiritually. I've watched them grow and get involved. Yet this year, I felt God telling me that it was time to step down. *But who will do it if I don't? What if they don't do it right? What if no one wants to do it? What if no one has the same commitment and concern?* This time I chose to be obedient. I told the nominating committee that I didn't want to be considered for that position. It was tough. And at this moment, I don't know if someone has accepted the position or what their goals and vision for the ministry will be. But I've made a conscious decision to trust God. If He wants the ministry to continue, then He will provide the right person and give them the vision and ideas He wants them to have. I know Him. I know I can trust Him.

Sometimes we forget that everything is not up to us. Ellen has to laugh at herself at times. When she hears of a need, she immediately tries to figure out how she can meet it or take the responsibility, many times knowing that she doesn't have the time, energy, or desire. Then God will fill it with someone else—someone who has the time, who sees it as a ministry, not just another thing to do, who does it better than she could've. Now she laughs at herself and wonders why she thought everything was up to her. It's not. God is in control.

3. *Ask yourself if this will be something that suits your gifts, talents, abilities, time, and goals.* God may be asking you to stretch and develop a new talent too. But He'll not ask you to do something that He won't give you all you need to do it with.

4. *If God doesn't lead you to say Yes, then just say No.* Don't make excuses. Don't feel guilty. Just say "No, I don't feel that's what God wants me to do right now" or "No, it's not something I feel I can do." Sometimes we're asked to do things we wouldn't enjoy doing. Or we know is not one of our gifts. Maybe we don't have the time. Maybe we need to save that time for our family.

We need to feel the freedom to follow God's leading and say No. At times it may mean disappointing people. Myrna hates to disappoint people or let them down. But recently she felt strongly that God wanted her to resign from a position she held in the church. She didn't understand why God was impressing her to resign and knew that people were counting on her, but finally she resigned—after months of being miserable while deciding if God really was asking her to resign or if it was just her idea. After she wrote her letter of resignation, God affirmed over and over that this is what He wanted—and opened a new door for Myrna that she really wanted. But in the meantime, people were disappointed. And they didn't understand. Some probably assumed wrong conclusions about why she had resigned. But Myrna was able to risk all of this in order to follow God's will. If it was God's will for her to resign, then He would take care of everything—and everyone.

Sometimes we have to say No to people and opportunities in order to say Yes to God. And we may not always understand why. Or even want to. But obedience brings us a freedom and joy that's worth saying No for.

At camp meeting this summer I was part of a skit for our family worship time. Eight children volunteered to help from the congregation. Each was given a sign, a plate, and something that went with the sign. I was given two dowel sticks. One at a time, each child walked out in front of me, showing the audience the sign they carried. Each sign had something written on it—something that is a part of many of our lives: family, exercise, healthy cooking, prayer meeting, Pathfinder leaders, etc. Then they showed the sign to me, offering me this role for my life. Each time I acted like I was thinking about it and then said Yes. Then they placed an object in my free hand that went with that role, like a baby for family, a pot for cooking, a hand weight for exercise. And placed a plate on one of the dowels and gave the plate a spin. I was supposed to keep the plates spinning (or at least act like I was; they didn't cooperate well) while my other arm quickly became loaded down with stuff.

After the eighth child gave me their object—I think it was the hoe for gardening—and walked away, I dropped everything except the Bible and read a verse reminding us that God will guide us in what to do.

All week afterward, people stopped me to say something about the skit. Kids would either point at me and say, "There's the lady who dropped everything!" or ask if everything was heavy. I guess they were trying to figure out why I had dropped it all. But adults knew. So many, especially the ladies, said, "That's how my life is!" or "That was so real."

But is that how God wants our lives? So full of things that we feel like we're juggling? That we're going to drop everything any minute?

Remember Psalm 23? God is our Shepherd. And the Shepherd makes His sheep lie down in green pastures. He leads them beside still water and restores their soul. To me this speaks of peace and quietness. Not rushing and busyness.

God promises to show us what to do, how to go. Proverbs 3:6, "In all your ways acknowledge Him, and He shall direct your paths." God will show you what to say No to and when to say Yes. He does want us to do things, to serve Him, but not to be so busy serving and doing that we don't have time for Him or for our families and friends.

My life is a lot simpler these days. Currently, I hold no offices in my local church. I still am involved behind the scenes here and there. I'm not always rushing somewhere or trying to get something done in time. And the world didn't end when I said No. Others filled in the gap. And I've been able to become more focused on the things that are really important to me. I'm doing a better job in the ministry I'm involved in because I can give it more time and focus.

And I have more time for my family. We've spent more time hiking. We're learning to canoe. We've read a pile of books and rode miles on our bikes. And it's amazing the conversations that pop up from nowhere when we're just hanging out together. And when I'm asked to do something, I take my time in answering. Praying about it first. Talking it over with Tim. I've realized I don't have to do everything. Just the things God wants me to. I'm learning to lie down in those green pastures and enjoy the still waters.

Reflection

1. How easy is it for you to say No? If you have a hard time saying No, ask yourself why. Why do you feel you need to say Yes?

2. What does your schedule look like? Are there things that need to go? Make a list of your priorities, in order (i.e., time with God, husband, children, friends, family, church, work, play, etc.). Compare this list to your schedule. Are your priorities reflected in your schedule? Are you spending time doing what is most important to you or the most urgent things?

3. Learn to say No, to prayerfully consider each thing asked of your time. What does God want? Ask for time to think and pray. Then pray. Trust God's leading.

Prayer _____

O Lord, teach me to number my days aright. Give me strength to prayerfully consider what You desire for me to do each day. Help me to include time for You, time to play, time to spend with those people who are important to me. Help me to trust You that You are in control and will get what You want done, through whom You desire. I don't have to do it all. Teach me to say Yes to you and No to the rest. In Jesus' name, amen.

seven

Am I Good Enough?

Have you ever felt as if you weren't good enough? You compared yourself to those around you and just came up lacking? Maybe you've felt as if you weren't pretty enough or tall enough or smart enough or successful enough. What does it mean to be good enough? Who decides what good enough is?

Marcie strives to get straight As in school. Bs aren't good enough. If it's not an A, Marcie feels she's failed, that she's dumb.

Laura feels uncomfortable attending women's retreats. She figures all the other ladies attending are spiritual giants. "I can't pray as beautifully as they do. I don't know my Bible as well. My devotional life is sporadic. I'm just not spiritual enough to attend," she says.

Megan works for a financial services company. As administrative assistant, she handles a lot of responsibilities, often with a lot of pressure. But when others in the office invite her to join them for lunch, she declines. "What would I talk about with them? They're higher in the company. They have their own offices. I'll never fit in with them."

Lea teaches in the children's department of her church. She's been teaching each week for several years and would like to take a break. "It's not that I don't like the kids. I love them. I enjoy being with them. But I wish I could be taught too." Her friends have encouraged her to turn down the position of teacher and join their adult class. "But I couldn't do that," she says. "They study all the time. I'm not that intellectual. Guess I'll stay in the children's class where things are simpler."

Barbara feels similar feelings. She is a part of an adult class at church and attends a weekly small group in the home of a church member. But she never says a word. She listens. And she has questions and thoughts in her head, but she's too afraid to share them. "I'm not as smart as everyone else. They all understand everything. I can't say anything."

Many of us wonder if we'll ever be good enough. We allow our feelings to keep us from being a part of the group, from reaching out to others, from sharing. We don't attend retreats, seminars, classes, social gatherings because we don't feel like we belong or fit in. We just don't feel like we're good enough.

Inside each of us is the basic need to feel as if we belong, to feel accepted, to feel good enough for someone to love. We need to feel our efforts are good enough, even when things don't turn out quite like we expected. We want to fit in because of who we are, not because of what we do or wear or say.

When we don't feel as if we're good enough, it often causes us to become competitive. We try to be better than others so we'll be good enough, liked, accepted. We copy people who we think are good enough. Or we just give up trying to fit in and stay home—or watch the group from the sidelines.

We know that God loves us just as we are and that He gives us value just by His love and the price He paid for us. He longs for each of us to find our value in Him and know that He alone makes us good enough. It's nothing that we do or say or have. Only Him.

Yet many of us, even as Christians, struggle to feel good enough, to feel valuable.

What makes you feel valuable? Where do you find your value?

In crossing off everything on your to-do list? In having a long list of accomplishments each day?

Joanne is pretty goal oriented. She's good at keeping lists. Each morning, she starts her list of things to do, and it's usually pretty long. During the day, if she does something that isn't on her list, she writes it down and then crosses it off. It gives her a sense of accomplishment at the end of the day to see all that she's done. It gives her a sense of value.

Tracie is someone who can accomplish a lot in one day. She gets up early in the morning and doesn't stop till late at night. She has a demanding job, two teenagers, a dog, three cats, and a husband who doesn't help out much at home. Not that she's asked him to. She says she doesn't mind doing it all. There's also the class she teaches at church. And she leads the social planning committee. Many weeks after church, she invites people home for dinner, which she stayed up till late preparing. "People are always asking, 'Wow, how do you accomplish so much?' Then they say they wish they could be more like me. I don't know. I get tired always running. And sometimes I wish someone would invite me over for dinner for a change. But I guess it does give me a sense of value. People admire me for accomplishing everything. What would they think if I suddenly stopped doing it all?"

And we do tend to value those who accomplish a lot. Those who hold many positions and do a lot of things in the church are valued and seen as leaders. But what about the quiet person in the background? Maybe they're a real prayer warrior for the Lord, yet no one knows. Maybe they have a quieter ministry. Maybe they send notes to those who are struggling. They may call shut-ins to check up on them. Their lists of accomplishments may not seem as big or as impressive as someone else's, but they're no less valuable to God. Their ministry is just as important. Mrs. Johnson calls and visits other elderly women in her church. Her phone calls and visits brighten many of their days. Miriam volunteers her time to teach art and sewing to seventh- and eighth-graders at her local church school. It's not just the fun they have in her class that makes them enjoy it, but it's the individual attention she gives each of them. She listens to them. Linda consistently prays for others. Her friends know they can count on her prayers. Quiet, behind-the-scenes ways of reaching out to others. People may never know what they do, but God knows and smiles.

If accomplishing everything on our to-do list makes us feel valuable, what about those days when things don't go according to plan and the to-do list still needs to be done by the end of the day? Can we still feel valuable? Can you spend the day playing with your children or visiting with friends or just reading a book and not cross anything off your to-do list and still feel good about yourself? Do you give yourself permission to relax and have fun—or is your value found in what you can accomplish each day?

Maybe you find your value in your job or your title. We can get so caught up in positions and titles. But in these days of downsizing and cutbacks, what happens when you lose your job or your title or position? What happens to your sense of value? Does it mean you're not good enough?

Nicole hates the inevitable question: "So what do you do?" She's a stay-at-home mom with two toddlers. "I know my decision to stay home was the right one. But when people ask me what I do or if I work, they mean do I have a 'real' job. Staying home is hard. But I wouldn't miss this time with my kids for anything. I praise God I can stay home. Money's tight and there are no extras, but the bills get paid. And I know a 'real' job wouldn't make me a better person. But it's hard saying I stay home. It doesn't sound as good as saying some impressive title."

Do you find your value in the things you own? A big house. Nice clothes. Or maybe you finally feel good enough because of your kids—their accomplishments, how cute they are, etc. Or possibly your looks give you a sense of value. Yet all these things are temporary. What happens to how you feel about yourself when things break around the house? Or your kids do something that goes against your values? Or you find a gray hair? Or gain a few pounds?

We need to find our value in God. In the value that He has given us, not in temporary things that change from day to day. We'll never be able to feel good about ourselves if our sense of self-worth is based on something that changes, something we can't control—even though we try and try and try.

God does value us. He has given us worth. To Him, we are good enough because He sees us through the blood of Jesus which covers all our sins, faults, bad habits, and areas we lack in. Nothing we can do will make Him love us more. He created us. It's His love that gives value. He bought us and paid the price for us. It cost Him greatly. Yet in His eyes, we are worth the cost. *You* are worth the cost.

I heard Ginny Allen share about a teddy bear she had bought at a secondhand store for $1. She planned to clean him up and give him away. She took him home and tossed him in the family room. The name on his tag caught her eye. One day at the library, she decided to look the name up in a collector's book. She found it and discovered that the teddy bear was worth hundreds of dollars. Immediately she moved him from the family room to a prominent place in the living room and placed him carefully on display. The teddy bear hadn't changed. What had changed was the value she saw in him. He had always had the same value. She just didn't know it at first.

We may not always really realize our value at first either. But when we take the time to look in the Book, we'll find that each of us has incredible value. God wants us to treat ourselves with the value He has given us. To live up to the value He has given us.

I read a story that tells of one person who learned to live up to her value—to the price paid for her. It's called "Johnny Lingo." The story takes place in a culture in which wives are secured by giving cows to their fathers. The girl that Johnny is pursuing is quite plain and very insecure. Her father knows that he will be fortunate to get even one cow for her, but he doesn't want to lose face. Johnny stuns the whole village when he offers 10 cows, an unheard-of price for any girl, let alone this one. They marry and move away. When they return some time later, she is a completely different woman—beautiful, talented, and full of poise. She became what her husband saw in her. The difference was in the value he placed on her. Johnny didn't just see something that the others could not see. He treated her according to the value he wanted her to have. She became a 10-cow wife because he treated her like one (*Putting Up With Mr. Right*, 74).

God paid an even more unheard-of price for us. He treats us according to the value He wants us to have. We can never really understand our value until we understand what it cost. How can we understand the cost? By studying the life of Jesus, especially the sacrifice He made on Calvary. Read the Gospel accounts of His persecution and death. Read books that tell of His sacrifice, like *The Desire of Ages*, especially the chapters entitled "It Is Finished" and "Calvary." Think about what Christ went through for you, for me—for each of us.

Both of my boys recently spent a week at camp. During worship each night the counselors portrayed a different part of Christ's life, with the last night being Christ's death on the cross and His resurrection. When I picked Zack up at camp, after showing me he could do a flip off the diving board, he said, "Mom, you would've cried if you were here last night."

"Why?"

"Because they showed Jesus dying on the cross; they used pancake syrup for blood. It was so real. It felt like I was there!"

"Did you cry, Zack?"

"No, I was too busy taking pictures."

All week he told people this same story, about how I would cry and about seeing "Jesus" die on the cross. He had always known that Jesus died on the cross. But seeing it made it more real. It touched his heart in a very real way. When I asked Joshua how God had revealed Himself to him at camp, he shared two things. The first was this portrayal of Jesus' death.

We can know that Jesus died for us. We can skim through the account in the Bible. But when it becomes real to us, when we can understand the agony, the pain, the true cost, we can understand more of the price paid for us and the value God has placed on us.

God paid the ultimate price for each of us. That price makes us treasures. Valuable. Are we willing to live up to that value?

God chose us to be His daughters because He loves us. I found this scripture, which spoke to me of God's love and paraphrased it a little: "For you are set apart as a daughter to the Lord your God; the Lord your God has chosen you to be a daughter for Himself, a special treasure above all else on the face of the earth.

"The Lord did not set His love on you nor choose you because you were great or important or beautiful or talented, or because you could accomplish a lot on His behalf, but because the Lord loves you and He will keep His promises, the Lord has brought you out with a mighty hand and redeemed you from sin.

"Therefore know that the Lord your God, He is God, the faithful God who keeps covenant and mercy for a thousand generations with those who love Him and keep His commandments" (Deuteronomy 7:6-9; my paraphrase).

God didn't choose us because we were good enough. We'll never be good enough on our own. There will always be something more to do, to achieve. There will always be someone else who can do it better or who is prettier or thinner. There will always be someone who won't be impressed or pay attention to us. God made us good enough with His love and the price He paid for us. You will always be good enough in His eyes, even when you fail or stumble. He sees the treasure in you. And He's willing to make that treasure shine. For Him.

Are you willing to begin living today good enough? Valuable? You are a special treasure to a heavenly Father.

Reflection

1. Do you ever struggle with feeling "good enough"? Are there specific areas or times?
2. What makes you feel valuable? Getting things accomplished? Your job? Home? If you lost it all one day, would you still have a sense of worth?
3. What is the cost God paid for you? Do you understand the cost? How will you help yourself to better understand the cost?
4. Are you willing to give God all your feelings of not being good enough and the sense of value that comes from anything except Him? Write out a prayer giving Him these things specifically.
5. How can you daily remind yourself of your value as God's daughter?

Prayer

O heavenly Father, thank You for the incredible price You've paid for me. For making me Your special treasure. Your daughter. Forgive me for not always seeing the value You've given me. Help me to daily understand what it cost You and to live up to the value Your love has given me. Help me to be good enough in You alone. Amen.

eight

In Quietness and Confidence

I was feeling exhausted. Our church had just completed its second evangelistic series, and as usual, Tim and I were totally involved. Always the last to leave each night. I had served as coordinator for the church this time; leading the committee, overseeing all the details. I had loved it. I enjoy organizing things and all the details. I even enjoyed the problems that came up—my adrenaline kicked in as I rushed around taking care of them.

As soon as the series was over, we had kicked off our efforts of shepherding the newly baptized members: helping them to become a part of our church family, helping them to feel accepted and loved, keeping an eye out for those who slowly stopped coming.

Then there was the local women's retreat. Not only did I organize, cook all the meals, and see to all the details, but I was the speaker too. That meant that I had to get all the talks and small group times together.

And, of course, there was everything else: housework, mothering, taking time for friends and my husband, plus all my other commitments such as church work, volunteer work, and helping at my son's school.

I was exhausted and overwhelmed. I realized that all my "doing" wasn't helping me to feel good about myself or who I was. It was just making me tired and causing me to feel even more inadequate. There were things I just wasn't getting done.

I needed rest.

Taking my Bible, I started searching scripture for what it said about rest. I looked up every verse that had the word *rest* in it. And looked up all the cross-references. And even some of the cross-references of some of the cross-references. I needed to find rest.

Two verses stood out for me. The first was Isaiah 30:15. "In returning and rest you shall be saved. In quietness and confidence shall be your strength."

"In returning and rest you shall be saved." My works weren't saving me. All the things I did weren't making me more of a Christian. Just more tired. In fact, the more I did, the less I knew God, because I had less and less time with Him. What did He want from me? Returning and rest.

God was calling me to return to Him, to return to spending time with Him. I've always attempted to have my quiet time in the early morning, while the rest of the house slept. Quietly, I would slip from bed and taking my worship basket, I'd go to the living room. Sometimes enjoying a cup of tea or cocoa, sometimes snuggled under a quilt, I'd spend time with my Father. The time was spent praying, journaling, studying, and reading—sometimes singing. It was a special time. And the more time I spent, the more special it became. But life had become so hectic that I wasn't able to get up in the morning. And if I did, my journal reflected my tiredness and that I didn't want to be up.

I tried having my time later in the day, but it didn't work. I'm a morning person. The best time for me is the morning.

Once I'm up and running, I'm running. I don't stop till I have everything done, or at least most everything. So it was hard for me to take a break and have my quiet time when I saw so much that needed to be done. So my quiet time was almost nonexistent. God wanted me to return to Him, to make my time with Him a priority in my life again.

He also wanted me to rest. Rest from trying so hard to do everything. Rest from trying to prove myself, trying to be important, trying to take care of everyone. Rest from trying to be the "perfect" Christian and just be. Be His. Allow Him to work in me and through me, instead of me trying to do it all.

"In quietness and confidence shall be your strength." My strength comes in quietness—before God and from busyness. That's how I can hear His voice and know what His will is. When I'm rushing in all the busyness, I don't hear a thing. I need to develop confidence, not in myself but in God. I can only find that confidence by spending time with Him and by listening to His voice and to His Word. The quietness and confidence come when I am returning and resting in Him.

In order to accomplish this verse in my life, I needed to change things. I needed to learn to say No. I needed to spend time consistently with God. I needed to turn to Him and not try to do it all on my own.

The second verse was also in Isaiah, chapter 32:17: "The work of righteousness will be peace, and the effect of righteousness quietness and assurance forever." This verse doesn't have the word *rest* in it. I found it during my times of cross-referencing. Righteousness comes from Christ—from our relationship with Him. As we surrender our lives to Him, He covers us with His righteousness. And His righteousness works in our lives, changing us.

His righteousness brings peace. Peace with who I am. Peace with what is happening in my life. As I trust Him, growing in

Him, I can let go. I can know that whatever happens to me or to those whom I love is for my good. I can know that God is a God who loves me, who doesn't allow circumstances that will destroy or harm me, even though they may be painful. Sometimes we shy away from pain. Usually when we pray for another person, we don't pray for painful circumstances to happen. Yet many times, painful circumstances are what bring about real growth and change in our lives. Christ's righteousness gives me peace during these times. Peace to trust that God is in control. It gives me peace to accept who I am in Him, to trust that He created me this way, and that He is still working, still molding me and changing me into what He desires me to be.

His righteousness brings quietness. Quietness from trying, from having to prove ourselves, from having to do all and be all. I can't do it. His righteousness brings me the ability to accept it and to rest in Him, to wait on Him.

His righteousness brings assurance forever—assurance of His love, His salvation, and His promises.

Peace, quietness, and assurance are all found in His right-eousness. And His righteousness is found in Him—in returning and resting in Him, in abiding in Him. The first step for me in growing in my self-esteem was learning to trust in Him, to make my relationship with Him the top priority of my day, to rest in Him, to allow Him to quiet my spirit, to find my peace and assurance in Him alone. Not in what other people thought. Not in what I could accomplish in a day. Just in Him.

Martha had to learn that. She, too, was a doer. It wasn't her doing that was the problem. It was her focus. Jesus had come to her home. They had been preparing for it all day, maybe for a couple of days. It wasn't the first time He would come to their home, but the first of many. When He came, Martha wanted to make sure everything was perfect. She fussed over every detail. And all the fussing and rushing was getting to her. Then she noticed that Mary was no longer in the kitchen. She was sitting at the feet of Jesus. Listening. I believe that Martha wanted to be there too. That she was jealous. Jealous that Mary could stop doing and sit and listen. But Martha saw all the things that needed to be done. Perfectly. Martha had lost her focus. She became so focused on serving that she forgot the One whom she was serving. Jesus didn't condemn her serving but her focus. "Martha, Martha, you are worried and anxious about many things." Her focus needed to be on Christ. There is a time when we each must sit at the Master's feet and listen. A time to take a break from the serving and doing. We need to be human *beings,* not human *doings.*

My friend Donna and I were talking about what was really important to us. What we wanted to be remembered for when we were gone. Donna wanted to be remembered as mattering to someone's life. That someone would miss her. That she would have added something special to her life. She also wanted to be remembered as a woman of God. Not as a worker. Not as the best organizer. Not as someone who was always dressed perfectly. Or who had the perfect home. She wanted to be remembered as a friend and a daughter of the King.

There are things more important than accomplishing everything on your to-do list. I've even thrown out my to-do lists. Each morning I tell God what my plans are; then I lay them at His feet and ask Him to accomplish His plans. Often I accomplish all that I wanted to. But God always adds other things to my plans. Like playing catch with the boys. Baking cookies together. Spending time with my husband talking and listening. Walking with a friend. Listening to someone whose phone call could be seen as an interruption in my plans but not His. Or spending the day praying and reading my Bible. I've given up my plans for His, so there's nothing to feel guilty about at the end of the day.

The housework will always be there. The job will be there in the morning. There will always be another meeting or committee at church. But moments with my Father, my family, and my friends are fleeting. It's in the quiet moments that I will find my greatest value.

Reflection

1. How does Isaiah 30:15 say we will be saved? Where is our strength? Where do you find your strength?
2. What is the result of Christ's righteousness in us? How can we experience peace in who we are? And have confidence and assurance? Are you experiencing these?
3. Have you learned to rest in Him? Or are you still focused on your doing? What can you do to change your focus? Pray and ask God to help you.

Prayer

O heavenly Father, thank You that in You I can find assurance of salvation, assurance in who I am, and peace to know that You love me and created me. Help me to return to You and rest in You each day. Quiet my spirit with Your love. Thank You, Father, in Jesus' name, amen.

nine

Waiting

Susan always thought it would be marriage. When she was married, with a place of her own, then she'd be happy. Peggy dreamed of the perfect house. When she got the home of her dreams, then she would be content. Emma knew her life would be perfect once she got that promotion. Her own office, a title; then she would feel important. For Jennifer, it was a baby. Once she had a baby, then she would be someone.

What are you waiting for to be happy and content? What will it take to make you finally feel important?

When I was in high school, I thought being a cheerleader would make me important. My life would be perfect. Each year, I tried out for the squad—in hopes of finally acquiring that status, the popularity that would make my life wonderful.

When I was older, I just knew I'd be secure and content and important if I had a title. A position would make me somebody. But becoming "Women's Ministries Director for the Pennsylvania Conference" didn't make me feel more secure in who I was.

"Maybe when I have some of my writing published, then I'll

feel good about who I am," I told myself. My first pieces were published as part of a women's devotional. It was kind of exciting to see something of mine in print finally. That had been my dream since I was a child. But still, it didn't change my attitudes about myself.

"When I get something published in a magazine, that'll be more real. Then I'll feel like I've arrived," I decided. The first article was beautifully laid out. I knew God had been involved in creating it. The background was light purple—purple was a signature color of mine. And there were sunflowers in the background. One of my best friends liked sunflowers—her kitchen was done in them and the article was on friendship. Seeing God's touch in the article's layout made me feel loved. And it was neat to think about people all over the country reading the article. But it didn't change how I felt about myself.

"OK, someday, if I ever get a book published, then I'll be confident. Secure. Somebody." And it's been exciting seeing the first book finished. A dream come true. That's been satisfying. To know that I persevered and completed it. Despite writing it, rewriting it, and then rewriting it again. It has strengthened me to know that I was assertive enough to even try. Me. An unknown. Seeing the book in print has made me feel good, but it hasn't really made me feel important. What has made me feel good about myself, even more confident about who I am, has been the process. The persevering. Not giving up. Submitting a second time to a new publisher after the first one rejected it. And I was only able to do it because of the strength I found in my relationship with God. I've learned that we can only wait expectantly on Him to make us feel better about ourselves.

A new house would be nice, but it won't change how we feel about ourselves. Marriage is wonderful and difficult at the same time. And we will grow in who we are as we grow in our marriages, but being married doesn't make you feel better about yourself. Neither will having a baby. Nor will a new job or a title or position. And losing a few pounds may help us to feel better about how we look, but it may not necessarily make us feel better about who we are.

We can wait on God alone to help us grow into secure, confident women. Psalm 62:5 says, "My soul, wait silently for God alone, for my expectation [or hope] is from Him." I've had to learn to wait on God alone. I've waited on a lot of things.

At times, I've waited on Tim to meet my needs, to make me feel good about myself—especially when I first started staying home full time with a new baby. When Tim got home at night, I wanted him to meet my needs. I'd been home all day alone with a baby. I wanted conversation. I wanted to go out. To do something. Tim had been at work all day. He had used up all his conversation and wanted quiet. He wanted to stay home, to putter around the house. I felt like my needs weren't being met. I was running on empty emotionally. Put that together with sleepless nights and a crying baby, and you have one unhappy person.

Even now, I often still wait for Tim to make me feel loved and accepted. And sometimes the waiting is long. Last week was an especially difficult week. He was frustrated. His company was downsizing. Responsibilities were changing. One of his favorite parts of his job was taken from him and moved to someone at corporate headquarters. And he didn't like how things were going at church. Every meeting was leaving him feeling angry. So he was silent, busy. When he did talk to me, his words were critical and short. I was crushed. In my journal, I told God I was feeling "empty and numb, foggy." I wanted Tim to make me feel loved, special, to bring me flowers, to talk with me.

That's when Janet called. (God always knows whom to send!) She's been a spiritual mentor to me. She's honest with me. "Tami, you're expecting things from Tim. That's wrong. You need to go to God to confess your expectations. Praise Him for how Tim is acting and ask Him what He wants to teach you through this."

Her words were hard to do. But I confessed my feelings to God. I praised Him for everything Tim had said and how it made me feel. Then I asked Him to teach me what He had for me in it. I believe with all my heart that God doesn't allow things to happen in our lives just to hurt us. And that nothing can happen to us without passing through Him. So God was allowing this for a purpose. (Janet suggested it was so this book could be better.)

And God reminded me that He alone is my expectation. He loves me already. No matter how anyone else—even Tim—acts toward me. I'm special to Him. I don't have to wait on Tim or anyone to make me feel loved. He's done it already. I just need to go to Him with my needs.

Who do you wait on? Or what are you waiting on?

Your husband. You long for him to take you out, to talk to you, to listen to you.

Marriage. If you could just find Mr. Right, life would be complete.

Your boss. For words of encouragement about the job you're doing.

A promotion or certain job. Then you'll feel as though you've arrived.

A friend. To call, to invite you to do something together, or maybe just someone to have as a friend.

Your children. To visit you, to appreciate all you've done and sacrificed for them.

A baby. Your maternal clock is ticking away. You can even picture what the nursery would look like.

A new house. If you just had more room. Or something newer.

The list could go on and on. And we keep waiting.

Psalm 62:4 tells us what we should do with our needs. "Trust in Him at all times, you people; pour out your heart before Him; God is a refuge for us. Selah." Trust Him and pour out your heart to Him.

Do you trust Him with your needs? Do you believe that He wants to meet your needs? Not just physical needs like protection and food, but even the smallest of all details, including that tiny need that may seem foolish to anyone else. Like a little bit of quiet during a busy day, just for you. A word of encouragement when it seems as though everything is going right—not wrong, and you really don't have anything to feel discouraged about.

One day I prayed for a dress. Tim had given me a dress for my birthday. He knew that I had liked a particular dress I had seen in a catalog. So on my birthday he told me to order it. And I did. Then I couldn't wait for it to come. But when I called they told me that the dress was on back-order for two months. I had planned on wearing it in two weeks. Disappointed, I asked them to send it anyway. A few days later I received a postcard telling me the dress would be shipped on a date two months away. What could I do? A few more days passed, and I was cleaning the house. That night I was going to my brother-in-law's graduation when a thought struck me; *I sure would like to wear that yellow dress.* So I prayed. I asked God to send the yellow dress that afternoon. As I thought about my prayer, I realized how selfish it had been. *Lord, I'm sorry for asking You to send that dress. How selfish! Please forgive me. I know it'd take a miracle to have the dress arrive today. And I know You love me enough to work a miracle for me, but never mind. I have plenty of things to wear, and I don't want to ask You for something so selfish.* I couldn't believe that I had been so selfish when there were so many more important things to ask God for. When I finished dusting, I went out to check the mail. And, of course, the yellow dress was there. In a box by the mailbox. It was even sent folded neatly on a hanger so it didn't need ironing. God's love for me is so much bigger than I can comprehend!

Now I'm not suggesting that everyone pray to God selfishly with their wish lists. But we need to know that God does care about every detail of our lives. Every thing that matters to us, matters to Him. He longs for us to talk to Him like a friend. Sharing from our heart. And He will bless. He won't say Yes to every prayer, but He will reveal His love in incredible ways. I can't wear that yellow dress without being reminded of His love. I smiled every time I passed the dress that afternoon.

I love this quote from *Steps to Christ*, 100:

> *Nothing that in any way concerns our peace is too small for Him to notice.* There is no chapter in our experience too dark for Him to read; there is no perplexity too difficult for Him to unravel. No calamity can befall the least of His children, no anxiety harass the soul, no joy cheer, no sincere prayer escape the lips, of which our Heavenly Father is unobservant, or in which He takes no immediate interest (emphasis mine).

Nothing that concerns us is too small for Him to care about. No detail too insignificant that He doesn't take an "immediate interest." Do you know God well enough to believe this? To know that He cares about everything that matters to you? *Everything!*

Trusting is the first part. Trusting comes from believing, from knowing God, from believing that He does care, that He does love you, that it does matter to Him.

Pouring out your heart to God is the second part. Telling Him what your needs are. Sharing every honest little detail, no matter how foolish or insignificant it may seem. God cares. He waits for you to tell Him so that He can take care of it. God is ready and willing to take care of every need of your heart. He's just waiting for you to give them to Him. Many times in my life, God has brought healing as I've poured my heart out to Him. As I've opened my heart to Him, He's been able to speak to me, to show me—always gently—my sin and selfishness. He's been able to take away the hurts and replace them with His love and peace. It's as I open up to Him that He can fill me and remind me that *He's* in control. I can find peace in that.

I've learned to pour out my heart to God. I've learned to

trust Him and believe that He really cares. I've prayed for reassurance that I'm doing what He wants me to. I've prayed for His encouragement to touch my heart somehow. And that He would open my heart to see His love on days that I felt unloved. Sometimes He's answered with a beautiful lesson from nature. A sunrise. Sun shining through the fog. A bird taking off from a silent pond just as I drove past. A flower poking up and blooming despite the cold and snow around it. Other times He's used a friend with just the words I've needed to hear. Or a song on the radio that spoke so clearly to my heart. At times, I've opened up His Word, and it's like the part I'm reading was written just for me, just at that time in my life. There have been times when I've poured out the anguish of my heart, crying and praying, and His answer has been in the peace that permeates me. And sometimes He's spoken quietly to my heart, his voice whispering His love and encouragement. But always He's answered. *Somehow.*

No person can meet all our needs. No material thing can make us feel better about ourselves. God can. "He *only* is my rock and my salvation; He is my defense; I shall not be moved" (Psalm 62:6; emphasis added).

What are you waiting for to make you happy? To make you finally feel good about who you are? To give you that sense of peace your heart desires? Are you waiting for something or someone who is temporary or faulty or who may never see your true need? Or are you waiting for a heavenly Father who loves you like no one else does, who longs to meet the needs of your heart, who longs for you to know the freedom and peace which only comes from living confidently in being His daughter?

Reflection _____

1. What are you waiting for to give you that sense of peace? To meet your needs? Can you complete this sentence:

When this happens_____, I'll
   be happy and content.

2. All too often, we wait for others to meet our needs. Who are
you waiting for? What needs of yours are going unmet? Are
you willing to give those needs to God? If Yes, then prayerfully give them to Him.

3. Do you trust God to meet your needs? How do you feel about
giving Him your needs? Do you believe that He really cares?
That He'll *really* do something about them?

4. How can you learn to trust God more?

Prayer _____

*Abba, Father, you know what I'm waiting for. I keep thinking that
when this finally happens, I'll be happy. Yet inside I know that real
peace comes from You alone. So I give You all that I'm waiting for. I
give You all my needs. And I willingly wait for You alone to meet my
needs. My hope and expectation comes from You alone. Help me to
trust You. Help me to let go and to wait on You. Teach me to wait. In
Jesus' name, amen.*

ten

Do We Really Want to Know?

Have you ever found that the closer you've grown to the Lord, the more sinful you seem? It can be so frustrating. You think things are going along pretty well. Your quiet time is meaningful. You're able to turn your thoughts to prayers more often through the day—keeping that attitude of prayer. You feel as though you know the way He wants you to serve, and you're doing it. Then—*wham!* It hits you. Maybe it's an attitude. Or motive. A weakness. And suddenly you're overwhelmed with your own sinfulness, how awful you really are.

As I've grown in Him, I've seen some pretty ugly sides of myself, things I didn't realize at first. Criticizing. Judging. Wrong attitudes and motives. There were times when I felt like giving up. I felt so hopeless. You'd think that the closer you grow to Him, the better you'd feel about yourself. But you begin to see even more of your own sinfulness, and it's not a pretty sight. Yet, we know that the closer we draw to Him, the better we know Him, the more He's going to shine in our lives. The more of His light will permeate our hearts. And light has a way of showing more flaws.

That's one reason candlelight dinners are nice. The soft, glimmer of light hides things. You don't see things as clearly. They say that's why candlelight dinners are so popular. The soft light is more becoming. It hides the lines, the gray, the flaws. It makes things look softer, nicer. Sitting by the fireplace in our living room, everything looks cozy and warm. But turn on all the lights and I can see cobwebs that need to be swept down (a hazard of living in the woods), and sock fuzz that needs vacuumed up. Walking in the dark, it's easy to not see the furniture sitting in your path. But turn on a flashlight and you can see everything in your way. In detail, if the light's strong enough.

That's how God is in our lives. When we first come to know Him, it's like a soft candlelight or cozy fire. But as we come closer to Him, His light shines brighter in our lives, revealing more and more of our real selves, our real motives, our real attitudes.

Sometimes as we grow closer to Him, we pray and ask Him to reveal to us our sins. As part of the Encounter Prayer, the person praying invites God to search her or his life and reveal any sins, then waits in silence, confessing the sins the Holy Spirit brings to mind.

But sometimes as we pray and ask God to reveal our sins, and He does, we focus on the sin and how awful we are. I know I have. I'll get so caught up in how awful I really am that I forget that God has forgiven me—and that I need to forgive myself. The next step in the Encounter Prayer is to thank God for His forgiveness of the confessed sin. The Bible promises us that God does forgive us of our sins. First John 1:9 is an often repeated verse, "If we confess our sins, He is faithful and just and will forgive us of our sins and cleanse us from all unrighteousness." Once we confess our sins, we need to let go of them, to accept God's forgiveness, to thank Him for it.

But the devil doesn't want us to forget how awful we are. He uses every opportunity he can to remind us of our unrighteousness. That includes reminding us of our sins. He dredges up things we've done from our past and tells us that we're bad, that there's really no hope for us. We'll never change.

But he's wrong. The Bible tells us that God forgives us. That He will change us. That *He* will complete the work in us. That's one of my favorite promises. Philippians 1:6, "Being confident of this very thing, that *He* who has begun a good work in you will complete it until the day of Jesus Christ." God will complete the work in each of us. He will change us and make us like Him. He has taken on the responsibility Himself. That's how much He loves us.

So when the devil reminds me of my sins, I don't listen. I say, "Yes, I did that, but God has forgiven me." And I remind myself that I'm forgiven and of the incredible grace of God. I once bought a T-shirt for my brother which read, "When the devil reminds you of your past, remind him of his future." The devil will lose the battle. But until it's over, he wants to discourage us so that we're useless to make a difference for God and we don't live with the freedom and joy that God desires for us to. But we don't have to listen to him. Our Father has taken care of us.

Another thing I've learned to do is praise God for revealing sin in my life. Sound weird? I praise Him for revealing the sin and thank Him for giving me the strength and courage to deal with the sin and win the victory. God doesn't reveal our sins to discourage us. When He reveals a sin to us, it's because He feels we're ready to deal with it. Because He's going to give us all we need to overcome that sin, to change and grow, to have a closer walk with Him.

One of the sins God has convicted me of is my judgmental attitude. This especially includes judging based on someone's appearance. I look at some people and totally forget that they're God's children too; that He loves them as much as He loves me. I form my opinions of them just by looking at them. Instead of trying to love them or see them as He does, I write some people off or don't go out of my way to befriend others. Just because of how they look or dress. That's wrong. And when God convicts me of it, I feel really bad. I even pray and ask God to give me a deeper sense of repentance. I want to understand how wrong it is. It's a continual prayer, because I haven't totally won the victory yet. Old habits are hard to break, especially old thought patterns. But each time God says, "Tami, you're judging that person by how they look. You're not seeing them as I do," I confess my sinfulness and ask God to forgive me and change my heart. And it's slowly happening. Just the fact that I'm more aware of that attitude helps. I can catch myself more often. I remind myself that God sees people from their hearts, not their outward appearance. I've highlighted 1 Samuel 16:7 in my Bible, "Do not look at his appearance or at the height of his stature . . . for the Lord does not see as man sees; for man looks at the outward appearance, but the Lord looks at the heart." I remind myself of this verse and pray that God will help me see what He sees.

Sometimes I'm tempted to feel bad about myself for falling into this sin again. But I turn those feelings over to God too. "*O Lord, I've done it again. Please forgive me. Please help me to change. I don't want to be like this! Help me to forgive myself, too, and to focus on You.*" God doesn't want us to beat ourselves up. When we do, we're again focusing on ourselves instead of Him. He wants us to let go of it, to cling to His forgiveness and His cleansing power.

God doesn't want us to feel guilty. He doesn't condemn us. He forgives us. "There is therefore now no condemnation to those who are in Christ Jesus, who do not walk according to the flesh, but according to the Spirit. For the law of the Spirit of life in Christ Jesus has made me free from the law of sin and death" (Romans 8:1, 2). Remember the words of Jesus to the woman caught in adultery? "Neither do I condemn you; go and sin no more" (John 8:11). He says those words to each of us as we come to Him in confession. "I don't condemn you. I don't want you to feel guilty. You're forgiven. Go on. And with Me and My strength, we'll overcome this sin."

We desire to grow closer to God. In order to do that, we have to let go of sin. To change and grow. And that can only happen as we allow God to reveal our sinful tendencies and attitudes, our sin. When we pray and ask Him to search our hearts, do we really want to know what He finds? We need to face what He finds with courage and thankfulness. Because God knows we're ready to deal with this part of our sinfulness. He will give us the strength and courage and ability to change, to overcome. We can praise Him for that. His light is shining brighter in our hearts and our lives. We are His victorious daughters.

Reflection

1. Do you allow God to search your heart and reveal your sins? How do you respond to what He reveals? Are you able to confess it as sin and then let go of it, claiming His forgiveness? Do you believe that He will change you?
2. How does God want us to respond to revealed sins? Does He want us to feel guilty? What can we do with that guilt?
3. Where is our focus when we don't forgive ourselves? How can we change that focus?

Prayer

O heavenly Father, thank You for the Holy Spirit, for the blood of Jesus shed to cover my sins; thank You for being my Father and Redeemer. Please "search me, O God, and know my heart; try me, and know my anxieties; and see if there is any wicked way in me, and lead me in the way everlasting" (Psalm 139:23, 24). (Wait and allow God to speak to your heart, confessing each sin.) *Thank You for Your forgiveness. Lead me to a deeper repentance and cleanse me of all my sin and sense of guilt and condemnation. Show me what You have for me instead. I praise You for being my Father and Faithful Friend. In Jesus' name, amen.*

The Encounter Prayer is taken from a booklet printed in 1988 by E-Van-gelism Publishing and was put together by Juanita Kretschmar. The steps of the Encounter Prayer are:

1. Ask God for His Holy Spirit (Luke 11:13).
2. Having claimed the protection He promised, worship Him!
3. Invite God to search your life (Psalm 139:23, 24).
4. Wait for His response. Confess the sins He reveals.
5. Thank Him aloud for forgiveness of the sin you confessed.
6. Ask God for the gift of an attitude of repentance concerning the just-forgiven sin.
7. Then thank Him for it.
8. Give God permission to reach deep within you and lift out all the guilt that accompanied the sin. That guilt is laid on His Son. Thank Jesus for releasing you—no matter how you feel.
9. Ask Him for what He will give you in exchange for the sin.
10. Then pray for others.
11. Make sure you spend the final time praising Him.

Claiming scripture is a big part of the Encounter Prayer also.

eleven

Daddy?
Father?

I was always Daddy's little girl. The oldest of five children and the only girl, I was Daddy's little girl. I can vaguely remember going to auctions with him when I was small—before the boys were old enough to go and take my place. I remember evenings spent in his room with him and two of my brothers, reading the Bible aloud. I remember the horse he bought supposedly for my birthday. (Really it was for him, but saying it was a birthday present prevented my mom from saying No.) I always knew my dad loved me and was proud of me. I always knew that he was someone I could count on, that no matter what happened in my life, I could go to him. He might not be happy with me, but he would never stop being my daddy. I trusted him. And growing up, I always planned to marry a man like my dad. He knew how to work hard. He knew the value of a dollar and always taught us to save, to only buy what we could pay for. He loved buying broken down things and fixing them up and reselling them for a profit. That's what he planned on doing when he retired. But he never got to retire. Six months before his retirement date, he suffered a ruptured brain aneursym and died. As I sat next to his hospital bed during those eleven days when he hung on unconsciously, I looked at those well-worn hands and the tanned face framed in graying hair and thought about this man. We hadn't always gotten along or agreed. But I had always been his daughter. His love was something I could count on, because I knew him. I knew what he was like. I knew that his love would always be there, that he would always want what was best for me. I knew my dad.

How well do we know our heavenly Father? To live like His daughter, we need to know Him, to be able to know what He's like. Is He Someone we can trust? Can we believe His words? Does He keep His promises? How faithful is His love?

Satan would like us not to know God. And he'll do anything to prevent us from knowing Him or from knowing Him like He is. Sometimes the devil shows us misconceptions of God. He wants us to believe that God is harsh, Someone we can't approach, who is waiting to judge us; waiting for us to do something wrong.

One friend shared that it was easy for her to love Jesus. "He's kind and loving and caring, but God . . . I just can't see Him like that. I picture the God of the Old Testament stern and harsh." Yet Jesus said that when we saw Him, we saw the Father. He reflected the Father in His life and character.

Mary went to a Bible study in her community. It wasn't her church, but she felt the need to study the Bible with others. During one of the first meetings, she was surprised by what the teacher taught: "God is awesome and powerful. He sits on His throne in heaven as the King of the universe. We can't approach Him. He is too mighty for us. We can talk to Jesus, but God is almighty. Not someone we can come to."

Satan would like us to believe that God isn't interested in our lives, that He's up on His throne in heaven waiting to judge us and that Jesus is begging for our lives, begging before a God that we can't approach. But God invites us to "come boldly to the throne of grace, that we may obtain mercy and find grace to help in time of need"

(Hebrew 4:16). God desires us to come before Him.

Sarah's afraid of God. She's not sure that she can trust Him. She couldn't trust her earthly father. He sexually abused Sarah from the time she was a little girl. The one who was supposed to protect her and make her world safe made her world a place of terror and confusion. Can she really trust God?

Cassie's dad was an alcoholic. He wasn't there much for her or her mom. When he was around, he was drunk and full of verbal assaults. He made her feel worthless and dumb. Her feelings toward her father spill over into her attitude toward God. Will He be there for her? Can she count on Him? Or will He just make her feel stupid?

"I grew up without a father," shares Brenda. "I don't know how to relate to a dad. Aren't they supposed to discipline? Be kind of stern? Be kind of distant?"

"My father was very strict. He wasn't affectionate. He never had time to play. He expected a lot from us, and when we didn't live up to his expectations, we knew it," Felisha says, and then pauses for a moment. "I guess I've always seen God like that too. Strict. Wanting me to live by His rules. Waiting for me to mess up so He could punish me."

Allison's dad was always a lot of fun. "He laughed a lot. And enjoyed playing practical jokes. There really weren't any rules. He let us do whatever we wanted. He never really got mad if we didn't come home when he asked us to. Isn't that what God's grace is all about? You know, loving and kind? Sure it'd be nice if we obeyed all the rules, but it doesn't really matter, does it?"

Many times, our attitude toward our earthly fathers colors how we see our heavenly Father. That's part of Satan's plan. He will do whatever it takes to prevent us from seeing God as a loving, faithful Father; Someone who is concerned about every part of our lives, Someone who has time for us, Someone that we can trust totally.

Joseph knew his heavenly Father. He had learned to trust Him totally, even when his brothers sold him into slavery and spent years in a dark prison cell, forgotten by everyone else. He knew that God was to be trusted. And when He was reunited with the same brothers who had sold him, he was able to say with confidence, "Do not therefore be grieved nor angry with yourselves because you sold me here; for God sent me before you to preserve life. . . . And God sent me before you to preserve a posterity for you in the earth, and to save your lives by a great deliverance. So now it was not you who sent me here, but God; and He has made me a father to Pharaoh, and lord of all his house, and a ruler throughout all the land of Egypt" (Genesis 45:5, 7, 8).

He knew that God was with him no matter how awful the circumstances looked and that God only wanted what was best for him.

How do we learn to know God like that? How do we learn to trust that God knows and does what's best for our lives—even if that means difficult times? How do we learn to know Him so well that we can trust that He created us to be exactly who He wanted us to be—all our quirks and faults included? How do we learn to *know* God?

By spending time with Him. It's the most obvious answer and sometimes the most pushed aside answer. We know that we need to spend time with Him, but . . . there are so many things to do. Urgent things. Important things. Time with God is important to us, but often it's the first thing to be skipped in a busy day.

Maybe we don't realize why we need to spend time with God. To many of us, our quiet time is another thing we're supposed to do. We know it's supposed to help us grow, help us to be better Christians. And we want to do it. But it's just another thing to do. And sometimes we're really not sure how to spend time with Him. We hear people talk about spending an hour each morning with Him and wonder, "What do you do for a whole hour?"

"I try to have my worship first thing in the morning," shared Susan as she walked with her friend. "I have everything I need in a basket and take it with me wherever I have my time with Him."

"Worship?" Jenny toyed with the word for a few minutes. "I've never thought of calling my time with Him 'worship.' It's just one of those things I should be doing and try to squeeze in the morning before the girls are up. But I wouldn't call the time I spend 'worship.' "

How about you? Is your time with God truly worshiping Him? Or are you just putting in time? Something that you should be doing? Why are you spending time with Him? Or, why *aren't* you spending time with Him? God wants it to be so much more than just another thing to do, another way to spend time. He longs for it to be worship—communion with Him. Time for friends; for a Father and His daughter to grow together.

How can we make our quiet time more worshipful, more meaningful? I'd like to share the things that have made my quiet time very special for me. I don't do all the things every day, but each one has been important to me at one time or another. Some of them, like journaling, I'd never give up.

Keep all your worship tools in one place. Everything you need, your Bible, a journal, pens, highlighters, devotional books, study books, whatever you think you'll need. Make the place attractive. I keep all my things in a big basket. That way it's easy to pick up and take with me wherever I choose to have my quiet time. A friend keeps all her things on a table in her living room next to the oversized chair she always sits in for worship.

Treat yourself to pretty things. A pretty journal. I'm enjoying journals with scripture verses on each page. I never bought them for myself before, but a church gave me one to thank me for speaking once, and it was such a blessing! All the scripture promises each day. Now I try to pick pretty ones for myself each time. Invest in nice highlighters and pens. I like to use fine point pens (often with purple ink) because it looks nicer when I write in the margin of my Bible. Medium points tend to bleed through the page. Have pretty bookmarks, good devotionals—whatever you enjoy.

Don't be afraid to vary your worship from day to day. Some days you may feel more like going for a walk and praying and singing. Some days you may want to journal and others you want to pray aloud. Don't feel that there's a step-by-step procedure you *have* to adhere to. Remember that worship is spending time with God, not a thing to be accomplished and crossed off your to-do list.

Include music. Sing. Listen to music. I find that playing my favorite CDs on the stereo throughout the day helps me to stay in a worshipful attitude. Music often ministers to my heart and turns my thoughts to God.

Share with a friend what you've learned. If something in your study excites you, tell someone. It will reinforce in you what you've learned and might be something exciting for someone else as well. My friend Sue and I often share what God is teaching us. She calls them "pearls." During our time together, we'll often share something we've learned from scripture or a lesson God taught us. We enjoy hearing what God is teaching the two of us. It reminds us how much a part of our lives He is and desires to be.

Find a prayer partner. I've been praying with Sue on Thursday mornings since April 1994. It's a time I guard and treasure. I've grown so much. We meet during her lunch hour in the building where she works. Her boss lets us use a conference room to meet in. We share what's been happening in our lives—our prayer requests, our struggles, our joys, our concerns. And then we spend a few minutes in prayer together. Sue's prayers and encouragement have helped me through some tough times. She also holds me accountable to commitments I've made to God and to my family and to commitments in using my gifts and in spending my time. I know that I can trust her. No matter what I share with her, she'll still love me. Sometimes I've confessed some pretty awful attitudes and motives to her. She doesn't gloss over them or put me down but prays with me and for me. And it's two-way. I encourage her and pray for her. I hold her accountable to the goals that she's set and to the ministry that God has for her. The Bible talks about friends being like iron sharpening iron. That's how I feel about my friendship with Sue. Like we're sharpening one another in our walk with God and in our lives and ministries.

If you don't have a prayer partner, pray and ask God for one. Then when He puts someone's name on your heart, ask that person if they would consider becoming your prayer partner. Choose a definite time and place when you'll pray together. It's good to have a set length of time and know about when you need to stop sharing and start praying before your time is up.

Vary your praying. Journal. Pray out loud. Try different "forms" of prayer. I love to pray through the steps of the sanctuary. There are many different forms—The Lord's Prayer, The ABC's of prayer, Encounter Prayer, etc. Occasionally, try a new form, making it fit your personality. Pray through scripture. Pick scripture to pray. There are several books that can help with this. One whole series is, *Praying God's Will for My* . . . There's one for husband, son, daughter, wife, etc. The author took scripture and rewrote it in the form of a prayer. Or you can use passages of scripture right from your Bible.

Spend time in thanksgiving and praise. This alone could change our prayer lives and our lives. Learning to praise God for who He is helps us to focus on Him instead of our problems. There have been times that praise has changed my attitude and outlook, though not the problem in my life. Yet somehow the problem no longer seemed insurmountable. When I praise God, focusing on who He is, I'm reminded of His character, that He will not allow anything that happens to me to harm me, that He always has my eternal good in mind, and that He is in control. There's nothing that happens that He can't stop or control. Praise helps us to keep our focus on Him and off ourselves and our trials and shortcomings.

Study the Bible, looking for who God is. One of the most exciting Bible studies I've done is looking for God in scripture. I began in Genesis with the plan of reading through the entire Bible from cover to cover, looking for what the Bible said about God. I figured that I'd get through Genesis pretty quickly—I've read it so often. I would study until I learned something about God and then stop and journal. The first day, I didn't even finish chapter one. The Bible reveals so much about God. A kind, loving God who is intimately involved in every aspect of His children's lives. I've found that the God of the Old Testament isn't different from Jesus in the New Testament. He is a God who defends and guides His children, doing whatever is necessary to draw them to Him. *It's important that our time with God include Bible study.* It's one of His ways of speaking to us. You can use a Bible study book or study a specific topic, word, or book of the Bible. Ask friends what has been helpful to them in studying the Bible. Sometimes I use a study guide. Other times I'll study a specific topic or word. Sometimes I just read a book of the Bible, reading until something stands out to me. Do a study on Jesus' miracles or His parables. Study different people in the Bible. I love studying about women in the Bible, imagining what their lives were like, how they responded to God in their lives. A book on manners and customs during that time period helps give some real insight.

There are many books that are helpful to read because they give us insights into the Bible, but never let any other book take the place of Bible study. I love to read and read as often as I can. But I choose not to read books during my worship time. I want God's Word to be my primary focus as I come before Him. It's too easy to just read what others say about God and His Word when we should be reading His Word for ourselves.

Keep a journal of what God has done for you. Even little things. God constantly told His people to remember. The word *remember* is used 148 times in the Bible. We need to remember how God has led us and what He's done for us. It will help us to trust Him, to be more confident that He is leading, and that He is involved in our lives. Keeping a journal of remembrance to read through from time to time can help remind us of who God is and how much He loves us.

I keep a "thanks" journal. Each morning I think of several things I can be thankful for from the day before. Some days it's hard. Other times it's incredibly easy. It's how I begin my quiet time. Entering His gates with thanksgiving. And it's a neat reminder to look back over.

Claim promises, making them your own. Several years ago, I chose a life verse. It was Philippians 1:6, "Being confident of this very thing, that He who has begun a good work in you will be faithful to complete it until the day of Jesus Christ." At the time, I was really struggling with whether I'd ever change and grow. This verse reminded me that *God* promised to complete the work—someday I would grow and change. I wasn't hopeless. Claiming promises, paraphrasing them in our own words, or putting our names in them makes His promises more real to us.

Sue has a promise box. Each morning she asks God to give her a promise for that day and pulls a promise from her box. Often she'll remind herself of the promise throughout the day, sometimes trying to memorize it. Lilly gave me a promise book. The promises are divided into sections according to needs and situations, making it easy to find a promise for what you are going through or feeling. One speaker shared at a women's retreat how she highlights all promises in one color. It makes them stand out and easy to find. Believe that God's promises are for you. Claim them. Write your name in them. Apply them to your life.

Recently I realized that God has given me special verses at

different times in my life. Verses that became prayers; promises I cling to. Like Philippians 1:6 when I feel hopeless. 2 Chronicles 20:17 when the battles just seem insurmountable. It was during that time that I began learning the importance of praise. I clung to Psalm 37:4 when things started happening in my life—good things, dreams fulfilled. The verse taught me what was the most important thing for me to do. And now Psalm 62:5 as I learn to wait on God alone. Some people choose a verse each year, praying and asking God to show them a special verse. Then all year, they pray this scripture, claiming it over and over. I realized that though I hadn't intentionally been doing this, God was doing it in my life. I can map a lot of the last few years of my life with the verses He has given.

Believe that God answers your *prayers.* When God answers a specific prayer for Sue or me, we'll often joke that He answered it because the other person prayed. But it didn't start out as a joke. Both Sue and I have faced times when we prayed for something but believed that God would answer someone else's prayer first because they were more spiritual than we were. We doubted that He would answer our prayers. We just weren't good enough. But God does answer our prayers. Being good enough or spiritual enough isn't a prerequisite. Faith is. Jesus said to pray believing that God would answer. Believe that God hears *your* prayers and answers *your* prayers. It may be helpful to keep a prayer notebook or journal with your prayer requests in it so that you can also record answers to prayer. I write prayer requests in blue and answers in pink. Some of the most exciting answers have been for those prayers that no one knew I was praying except God. It reminded me even more that God does answer *my* prayers.

We need to believe that God does hear our prayers, that His promises are for us, that He does desire to spend time with us. We are His daughters.

One day as I read *The Desire of Ages*, I came across this quote,

"The Voice which spoke to Jesus says to every believing soul, 'This is My beloved child, in whom I am well pleased.' " In my mind I imagined God saying this over me, "This is My beloved daughter, Tami, in whom I am well pleased." It was hard for me to picture God being pleased with me. I mess up so much. I fail. Let Him down. Struggle. But as I thought of my own sons, even though they don't always behave the way I want, even though they argue and fight and disobey, I love them. They bring joy to my heart. God looks at me and sees His daughter. And even though I disobey and fail Him, I bring Him joy. It's hard to believe or comprehend unless I look through the eyes of a Father seeing His daughter.

When Joshua came home from camp one summer, he brought Tim and me each a gift. Sun catchers. We had given him a little spending money, thinking he would buy something for himself. But he chose to buy something for each of us. One was brightly colored with flowers and a cute saying. The other was plainer. That was the one he gave me. As I hung it in my kitchen window above the sink, I looked at it. A creamy white dove with red and blue in the background. The words from *The Desire of Ages* repeated themselves in my thoughts: "This is My beloved child, in whom I am well pleased." The sun catcher is a daily reminder that I am His daughter. Beloved. Bringing Him joy.

Daily I seek to know my Father better. And as I've learned to know My Father better, I've learned to trust Him with who I am.

Reflection

1. How do you picture God? Write down a description. How do you see Jesus? Is it different than how you view God? If it is, why?
2. What is your feeling about spending quiet time alone with God?

- It's something that I should do, but I'm not. I don't know how to start.
- It's something that I want to do, but I just can't seem to find time.
- It's something that I do for a few minutes each day because I should.
- It's a time that I look forward to every day.
- Not only do I look forward to it, but I don't let anything take its place.
- For me, it's just putting in time.
- It feels like I'm really worshiping God! That He's teaching me and leading me.
- I have my good days and my bad days.

3. Now go back through the above statements. Which one would you *like* to be your answer? What can you do, beginning today, to make that possible?

4. Fill in your name and read it often:

"This is_____, My beloved daughter, in whom I am well pleased!" says God.

Prayer _____

O Gracious Father, thank You that I am Your daughter. Thank You for loving me and for being pleased with who I am. Help me to spend time with You each day, getting to know You better and living more like Your daughter. In Jesus' name, amen.

twelve

Growing Up

The truth about low self-esteem is where our focus is. Low self-esteem is focusing on us. On what we're not doing or can't do. We don't always realize that. We know when we hear someone bragging about themselves where their focus is. But we fail to realize that when we're constantly putting ourselves down and feeling inferior to everyone, we're focusing on ourselves too. And that's not where our focus should be.

Our focus should be on God—on what He can do and desires for us; on who He is and on all that He is willing to do in us, through us, and for us. His Word is full of His promises to us. As we grow in Him, growing up as His daughters, we will learn to focus on Him, not ourselves, and to claim His Word as true for us.

Psalm 34:4, 5 pretty much sums up what growing in Him is. "I sought the Lord, and He heard me, and delivered me from all my fears [my insecurities and feelings of inadequacy]. They looked to Him and were radiant, and their faces were not ashamed."

First, we seek Him. Then He hears us and changes us. And as we look to Him—focus on *Him*, not *ourselves*—we will become radiant. *Radiant!* And we won't need to be ashamed of who we are. No more trying to please others and seeking their approval and encouragement. We will be radiant because we will be reflecting our Father.

One way we can know we're reflecting Him is when we reflect His character, when His fruit is evident in our lives. "But the fruit of the Spirit is love, joy, peace, longsuffering, kindness, goodness, faithfulness, gentleness, self-control" (Galatians 5:22, 23).

Is His fruit evident in your life, not only in how you treat others but in how you treat yourself as His daughter?

Can you love whom He has created you to be—just as you are, right now? That doesn't mean that you won't change and grow, but it means loving yourself and accepting yourself right now and not waiting till you've become the person you think you should be.

Do you experience joy in being you? In watching Him grow in you? I'm learning to. I'm learning to feel a real joy in seeing who He's making me to be. When I do something I never thought I could—even something as simple as starting conversations with women I don't know at a retreat—I get excited to see what He's doing in my life. I begin to feel good about me because of Him in me.

Do you have peace with who you are? Or are you constantly trying to be someone else? Can you be patient with yourself and allow yourself to make mistakes? Sometimes we think we should be perfect. But we're not. Sally tried to learn to ski. She concentrated and listened carefully to every word of the instructor. She tried following everything he said. Whenever she fell or made a mistake, she got mad, "Stupid, you're never going to learn! Try harder!" But when she took her son, Michael, skiing for the first time, things were different. When Michael fell, she gently helped him up, saying, "Good try, Michael! You're really getting it." Each mistake was met with a word of encouragement and a gentle touch or hug. By the end of the day, Michael was doing pretty well on the slopes. Sally had patience with Michael. She didn't expect him to do it perfectly the first time. When he fell, she expected it. She encouraged him and helped him up. But she wasn't that way with herself. Why not? Why can't we be patient and expect that we'll make mistakes, fall down, and have to get up and try again? It's OK.

Are you kind to yourself? Are you gentle with the words you speak to yourself, with your expectations and time? My friend Minda and I were just talking about doing things for ourselves. So often we take care of everyone else that we fail to take care of ourselves. It sometimes comes to the point that we can't accept gifts and nice things for ourselves. She had been watching a program, and several ladies were talking about how when they receive nice things, they don't use them. They put them away for something special. And for most of them there was never anything special enough, so the things had been sitting in closets collecting dust.

Sometimes being kind to ourselves means taking a few minutes each day to do something for us. Tanya and I try to keep each other accountable to doing this. When we talk to each other during the week, inevitably one of us will ask, "So, what have you done for yourself today?" For us, it may involve spending time reading or going for a walk or taking a trip to the craft shop with no kids or even a bubble bath. Other things we can do for ourselves may include not bringing work home at the end of the day but enjoying the evening with your family instead. Perhaps its calling a friend you haven't talked to in a while, going out for dinner instead of cooking, or picking up takeout on the way home. It could be saying No to overtime or going out to lunch instead of trying to clear the pile of work on your desk. We need to be kind to ourselves. It will help us to feel refreshed. Give us more energy to reach out to others. It's hard to reach out when you're burned out.

Are you faithful to yourself? Faithful in taking time to grow and forgive yourself? Faithful in not speaking unkind words about yourself in front of others? Have you learned self-control, even in how you think about yourself?

As we grow in Him, we will fall. We will still have to deal with insecurities, self-doubts, the urge to please and to prove. But we can learn ways of dealing with our insecurities. We can plan ahead of time how we will react when they assail us.

When we're tempted to worry about what others think of us, we can do a couple of things:

First, trust God. Trust Him with what others think about you. He's the only one who can change what they think. You can't, no matter how hard you try. Remember that when you gave Him all of you, you gave Him your reputation. He's responsible for what others think. It may be hard to let go and trust Him—especially when others misunderstand—but He will take care of it. Psalm 37:5, 6 says, "Commit your way to the Lord, trust also in Him, and He shall bring it to pass. He shall bring forth your righteousness as the light, and your justice as the noonday." Trust Him. He will let people see what He wants them to see. Sometimes it may take time. Sometimes people may never fully understand. That's OK. He'll allow what's best.

You can pray that God will help others to think the way He wants them to. I continually pray that God will give Tim the attitude He desires him to have toward my ministry. And God has worked it in some pretty amazing ways. Tim has not only been supportive, but he has been a big help by going with me to places and offering suggestions. Yesterday on our way back from a tea with women's ministries leaders in the central part of our state, he even asked what I did at the teas and how it went. I knew he actually listened, because he offered some suggestions and insights as I shared some of the things that happened and were said.

Remember that people don't think about you as much as you're afraid they do. In fact, they may be wondering and worrying about what you think of them. Leo Schreven shares in his book, *Cowboys Make Better Preachers*, that we don't need to worry about what others are thinking of us "because they're not thinking about (us). They are wondering what (we) are thinking about them."

Sometimes we feel worthless and hopeless. God doesn't want us to feel that way. It's not how He sees us. He sees us through Jesus, so He sees us as His perfect daughters. We can learn to put off these feelings of worthlessness and hopelessness too.

Remind yourself of your value in Christ. God paid an incredible price for you. And He wants us to see ourselves through that price—through the value that Christ's life gives us.

Repeat scripture that reminds you of God's love. The Bible is full of God's message of love and hope. Memorize scripture. Highlight it. Keep notecards with special verses handy to read when you need a reminder.

Realize that your focus is on you and not on Him. Look past yourself and remind yourself of who God is, of all He wants to do for you and all He is doing in your life. Praise Him for who He is and for His love for you. Focus on Him and His adequacy. Study His names and their meanings, thinking how that part of Him reflected in His name has touched your life. Praise Him using His names and the character they show. Praise is a powerful way of changing our focus from ourselves to God, because it gets us thinking of who He is.

Pray and give your feelings to God. Tell Him how you feel. Be honest. He can't bring healing for our feelings if we don't trust Him with those feelings in the first place. You don't have to sugarcoat it. God already knows. And if some of what you're feeling is accurate and there is something you need to change, ask God for the strength and courage to change, and then trust that He has already begun to work. Give Him your feelings. He doesn't want you burdened with them. I recently read that we're His sheep, and sheep aren't beasts of burden. God doesn't want us to carry around feelings of worthlessness and hopelessness. He wants us to experience joy and peace. Accept His joy and peace. Praise Him for it.

Sometimes our insecurities cause us to be too sensitive. We take things personally and sometimes get on the defensive. But God can help us to see the situation more realistically and to respond in a positive way.

Step back and look at the situation again. Was there a reason for those people to respond to you the way they did? If there is, make amends. If not, prayerfully consider why they said or did what they did. Did they really mean what they said the way you heard it? Could there be something else happening in their life that caused them to respond to you the way they did? Maybe they're having a bad day. Maybe there's a struggle they're facing right now. Realize that not everything happens because of you.

Ask God to help you see things clearly and to respond the way you should. Give Him your feelings and the way you want to respond. Remember that sometimes giving something to God means giving it to Him again and again—not because He doesn't take it but because we don't give it totally.

Sometimes we say Yes to too many things. We don't want to let people down. We want to live up to their expectations for us. Or we may get a sense of importance or belonging by saying Yes. But we need to learn to say No. We're not human *doings* but human *beings*. We need time to *be*. To be who God wants us to be.

Prayerfully consider what you should do. Ask God. Then wait for His answer. Ask yourself why you're saying Yes. Is it for the right reason—because God wants you to—or for another reason? What will happen if you say No? If God wants something done, He'll get it done.

We also need to learn to accept how we look. We can do things to make us feel better about ourselves. And we need to do things to make our lives healthier, such as eating right, exercising, and getting enough rest. If you feel you need to make changes, set realistic goals. Give yourself time. Let go of the things you can't change or don't want to put forth the effort to change. Get a friend to help you stay accountable.

Sometimes our insecurities can cause us to be perfectionists. We're afraid to try anything we might not do perfectly. We beat ourselves up for mistakes.

Give yourself permission to fail. God does. He loves you no matter what. It doesn't matter if it's perfect or if you fail. Sometimes we need to fail in order to learn. Sometimes we need to risk failure if we want to try to succeed.

Trust God with the results. As you pray and give God each situation and part of your life, trust that however it turns out, He is in control. It's the way He wants it.

As we grow in Him, we'll still slip into old habits. We'll still put ourselves down and worry about what others think. But as we learn and change, the old way of reacting won't happen as often, or for as long a duration, as we learn new ways of dealing with the thoughts and feelings. The most important thing is to never give up, to keep heading in the right direction, to not allow a defeat to stop us, to turn to Him, to focus on His love instead of our weakness.

I'm learning to. My journal entry from September 25, 1996, reflects some growth. Instead of putting myself down, I turned to God.

Here I am, Lord.

I've fought with Tim. Spent money unwisely. Ate too much junk. Didn't get up in time for time with You. And I'm ready to cry at the drop of a hat.

But You love me still. O, Father!

Thank You!

For loving me. For always being there. For always working in me.

Father, fill me with Your presence and Your faith . . . (let my life) bring You glory . . . .

I love You, Lord. Let Your love pour out of me.
In Jesus' name, amen.

Reflection _____

1. What can you do when the insecurities and old habits and downtalk happen? (And it will.) What can you do about:
   • Seeking other's approval
   • Wanting to be important
   • Putting off compliments
   • Worrying about what others think
   • Being too sensitive? Taking things personally? Being easily defensive
   • Not trying new things? Feeling like you have to do everything perfectly? Never wanting to fail
   • Telling yourself you're dumb, lazy, you blew it, etc.
   • When you hear other voices telling us negative things about ourselves
   • When you beat yourself up after you've done something?
   • Not being able to say No
   • When appearance matters too much

Prayer _____

O Lord, I fail. I know it. And I feel bad about myself. Help me to learn new ways to respond. Help me to learn to like myself, to like who You made me to be. Help me to find my confidence in You alone—not from others or from my accomplishments. Help me to learn to live as if I really believe that I'm Your daughter. In Jesus' name, amen.

thirteen

Our Heart's Desire

She stood before the congregation and sang the song she had practiced. Music blared loudly over the PA system. Some of the older people fidgeted in their seats. One excused herself to go to the restroom. She was uncomfortable with the type of music being shared and felt it was better for her to leave the sanctuary than to sit and allow her critical thoughts to grow.

I should've followed her example. But instead, I sat there and went through my "list." *Her dress is too short. And a tank top! Why would she wear something so revealing when she knew that she would sing special music? She could've at least stood behind the pulpit. And the music! I enjoy that song when I'm vacuuming, but for worship? There are rules about that here. Why doesn't anyone enforce the rules?* On and on my mind went. I had lost any possibility of a blessing. I was too busy judging the young teen who was attempting to praise God.

I found myself reflecting on the situation later that week with a friend. She, too, hadn't liked the music or the outfit and had sat critically during the special music. We both knew it was wrong to judge and that we shouldn't be so critical. But we weren't sure how to handle this situation. How did we stop these negative thoughts?

"See her as I do." God nudged my heart. How did God see her? I went through the morning worship again in my mind. What did God see?

I believe that God saw a young woman who wasn't sure where she belonged. She was too old to be with the "kids" but too young to fit in with the "grown-ups." She wanted so much to be grown up and to fit in, to belong. When she'd been asked to sing special music, she'd been excited. "The church is letting me be involved!" She picked a song that was special to her. She practiced over and over in front of the mirror. She sincerely wanted it to sound good. That Sabbath morning she had picked an outfit that made her feel more grown-up. She had taken extra pains with her appearance. She practiced her song on the way to church. When the time came for her to sing, she nervously went forward. "Help me, Lord!" she silently prayed. She wanted it to be special.

God sees us differently than we see ourselves, or than we see others. My friend and I had judged this young woman on her outward appearance. God saw her heart. He knew that she loved Him, that she longed to please Him. He knew her insecurities and fears. Her song was a blessing to Him but not to us. We were too busy seeing the negative.

It happened in the Bible too.

It was time to anoint a king. Samuel, the prophet, followed God's directions and went to the family of Jesse in Bethlehem. When the oldest son came forward, Samuel said, "Surely, this is the one!" He was tall and handsome. He looked like a king. But God said No. As each son passed, God said No. Then the youngest son was called for. He came running, hair flying wildly, cheeks ruddy. He smelled of sheep. There was a sparkle in his eye, a tenderness in his look—but was he king material? No one thought so. He was the youngest—not the oldest or the biggest or the strongest. He was a young shepherd. But God saw past David's outward appearance and saw a heart full of praise and love for his God. He saw a young man who desired to live his life for God. And as David grew older, he made mistakes. Big ones. Ones we might never think of committing. God still saw David as a man after His heart. That's because God looked past David's outside—even the sins—and saw a heart that desired to live completely for God. A heart that was willing to be molded, was soft and ready to repent.

And that's how God sees each of us. He looks past our outward appearance, past our mistakes and our sins, our bad habits and faults. Past our successes and our strengths and abilities. And He sees our heart's desires. He knows that we long to grow in Him. We long to know Him better. We want to spend time with Him. We want to serve Him.

Deuteronomy 7:6-9 (my paraphrase) says, "For you are set apart as a daughter to the Lord your God; the Lord your God has chosen you to be a daughter for Himself, a special treasure above all else on the face of the earth. The Lord did not set His love on you nor choose you because you were great or important or beautiful or talented or because you could accomplish a lot on His behalf but because the Lord loves you and He will keep His promises, the Lord has brought you out with a mighty hand and redeemed you from sin. Therefore know that the Lord your God, He is God, the faithful God who keeps covenant and mercy for a thousand generations with those who love Him and keep His commandments."

It's not who you are or what you do that causes the Lord to love you. It's just *you*. He looks past all that you do—whether good or bad—and sees your heart. What is your heart's desire today?

Psalm 37:4 promises, "Delight yourself in the Lord, and He shall give you the desires of your heart." As we grow in the Lord, delighting in spending time with Him, He will give us the desires of our heart.

I couldn't believe that she had compared me to Janet. I even wrote it in my journal as I thanked God for her encouragement. *Thank You, Lord, for Lois's telephone call. It was such an encouragement to me. She really does have the gift of encouragement! But can you believe that she said I'm like Janet? How I wish I was! I'll never be the woman of prayer that Janet is. I'll never be as spiritual and wise.*

Later that week during my quiet time, I was reading through the last week's journal entries. My journal is full of prayers written like letters to God. When I came across this entry, God stopped me and spoke to my heart.

"When I see Janet, Tami, what do I see?"

I thought for a moment. I knew what I saw. I admired her so much. She had taught me so much. But if God looked on the heart, what did He see in Janet's heart?

"Lord, You must see a woman who is completely devoted to You. Who longs to serve You and please. She desires for others to know You more completely. You see a heart who loves You above all else."

"Tami, what do I see when I look at you?" God gently asked.

Again I thought for a moment. I knew what I saw. It wasn't all pretty. But what did God see when He looked at my heart?

"Lord, you see a woman who loves You completely and who desires to serve You and please You more than anything else! And who wants to share Your love with others."

God nudged my thoughts. "Do you see the similarities?"

My heart soared as I realized the lesson that God was teaching me. When I looked at Janet and at others, I too often compared myself with their outward accomplishments. Their spiritual depth and their successes. Then I looked at my own faults and insecurities. (Why do we never look at our strengths and successes?) I never measured up. It made me feel even more insecure.

But when God looks at us, He sees past all the outward things we see and looks at hearts who love Him, who long to be close to Him and to share His love with others. He sees women who are more equal than we think, women who share a love for Christ and a heart for service. Our accomplishments really don't matter. There is no need to try harder or to impress. We can rest securely in God and allow Him to lead.

God wants us to rest in Him, to trust Him with who we are, to not focus on what we or others accomplish but who He is and allow Him to work through us.

In Genesis 1, as God began creating each tree and plant, He created them each to produce according to their kind. He created us in the same way. He desires us to serve Him in the way He created us, with the gifts and talents He gave us. He doesn't want us to serve like someone else or compare ourselves with others and find ourselves lacking. He desires us just the way we are.

Sometimes our insecurities paralyze us from doing things. One woman said, "I never went to women's retreats, because I assumed everyone else was more spiritual. I pictured everyone else being these spiritual giants, and I knew I wasn't. Now that I'm here, I've learned that we're all pretty much the same—struggling, rejoicing. Some of us may know how to pray better or study more, but we're each struggling with who we are, what we're supposed to be doing, and why we're not as good as someone else."

Hebrews 12:1 tells us to throw off all that hinders our walk with Christ. This includes our insecurities. The fears that paralyze us from doing what God has called us to do. The doubts that stop us from living like the daughters He has made us to be.

God wants us to be able to live without the burden of constantly feeling down on ourselves, of always questioning ourselves and doubting what we do. He wants us to be free from comparing ourselves to others and coming up short. He made each of us unique, each of us to fill a certain part in His plan.

My two sons are so different. Joshua is calm and levelheaded. He has a wonderful gift for music. His voice is so sweet and sincere. He can listen to the choir practice and pick out each part and sing. He does what he's told to do quickly, without much complaining. Trying to do the best he can.

Zachary is a charmer. One minute he can be delightful and so funny; the next he's stubborn and demands to have his way. He loves to sing and hum, and he can draw wonderfully and has quite the imagination. But he'd rather not work if he's not forced to and will tell you so. He complains a lot. And hugs a lot. He loves to snuggle and talk. His brother is quieter, and never really shows that he'd like attention or to snuggle, though I know he does.

Do I love one more than the other? Do I think that one is better than the other?

Never! I love both of them individually for who they are. I encourage each one of them in their gifts and discipline each one differently—according to his own needs and personality. When I spend time with them individually, we spend that time in different ways. The prayer requests I have for each of them are different in many ways.

Does God do any differently with His children? No. He loves each of us for who we are. In fact, He created us to be who we are. He chose the gifts, personality, character, and abilities each one of us was to have. He disciplines and teaches each one of us in the way that will be best for us. And He calls each one of us to serve Him in the way He has for us.

Being His daughter does mean serving. It means using our

gifts to meet the needs of others. Maybe we don't know what our gifts are. How can we find out?

There are spiritual gift tests that churches often offer or are able to offer. Check with your pastor about the possibility of having a spiritual gifts seminar in your church.

Ask others what they see in you. Many times our friends can more clearly see our abilities. I can see certain gifts in my friends. Lois and Sue have the gift of encouragement. Deb and Bill have the gift of helps. My mom, who says that she doesn't have any gift, also has the gift of helps and of hospitality. Don't look down on the gifts you have because they're not as "great" as someone else's. God needs *all* our gifts combined to finish His work.

Think about what you enjoy doing. Is it working with children? Teaching? Having people over to your home? God gave us our gifts not only to serve Him but for us to enjoy. Do what you enjoy doing for Him. Cecelia loves flowers and digging in the dirt. Each spring she puts this love into service by planting beautiful flower beds for the church. Whenever I pass them, I think of her and her love for flowers and their colors.

Be willing to try different things. Help in different areas in your church or community. If you find that what you've tried isn't for you, then quit—*without guilt.* You haven't failed; you've succeeded in finding something that isn't for you.

As you serve Him by serving others, try not to worry about what others are thinking of you. God doesn't want us to serve Him to look important or to make others approve of us. There are times in my life that doing what He asked meant quite the opposite.

I was once asked to serve in a position that I felt God had opened for me. I was really excited about the possibilities until I heard what someone was saying. A woman was spreading rumors that I was unfit to serve in that position. She attacked my character and said that I wasn't a good Christian woman, nor was I submissive to my husband—all things that I strove to do. I was crushed. For a week I cried and searched my Bible for answers. I wanted to quit! "I'm not doing it," I cried to Tim, "I'm telling the board I quit! I can't take these rumors that she's spreading."

"Tami, don't let the devil win. Didn't you feel that God wanted you to take this position?" Tim was patient.

"Yes, but look at what she's saying about me," I cried. What other people thought was so important to me and she was telling others these awful things!

"Trust God to take care of that. He's in charge of what other people think about you. He's asked you to do this. Are you going to be obedient to Him? Or are you going to be disobedient because of what someone is saying about you?" Hard questions. I believe that part of our job as Christian husbands and wives and friends is to ask the hard questions, to hold one another accountable in our spiritual walk.

And Tim was right. I needed to be obedient to God no matter what people said or thought. I served in that position for six years. It opened the doors for me to serve more effectively in women's ministries on a conference level, providing experience and ideas that I could share with local coordinators. If I had quit, I wouldn't have been able to do what I'm doing now.

(And later that very woman came and complimented me on the ministry I was leading and affirmed me as a mother! God had changed how she saw me. I had given Him my reputation, and He had defended me.)

If your heart's desire is to serve God, to truly live like His daughter, then lay your insecurities, self-doubt, and inadequacies at His feet. Use the gifts and abilities He has given you with joy and confidence in Him, serving no matter what others think or no matter what you think others think. Delight in Him, and trust that He will give you the desires of your heart.

Reflection

1. What is your heart's desire? Spend some time in thought and prayer, searching to see what you truly desire.
2. What have your insecurities and fears kept you from doing? Are there feelings that are hindering your walk with Christ?
3. What are the gifts and abilities that God has given you? Write them down. Pray and thank God for each one, asking Him to show you how to use this gift in the way He desires. If you don't know what your gifts are, try at least one of the suggestions to determine what they may be.
4. Have there been times, or currently are there times, when you are more concerned about what people thought about you than doing what God was asking you to do? How can you change that?

Prayer

Father, You know my heart's desire! How I long to totally be Your daughter. Teach me to delight in You, trusting You to take care of those desires, helping me to grow in You. Help me to throw off all that hinders my walk with You, showing me how to serve You in the unique way You have for me. Give me joy in serving You as the daughter You have made me to be. In Jesus' name, amen.

fourteen

Self-Esteem Versus God-Esteem

Lilly and I were talking about the ideas in this book as I prepared the material for a seminar. I was sharing with her my realization that my low self-esteem was really me focusing on self, not on God. And I wanted to see myself through God's eyes with the value He has given me. I wanted to feel good about me and to accept myself.

"All this talk about self-esteem," Lilly said. "We're supposed to help our kids have good self-esteem. We need good self-esteem. I think to feel good about who we are, we need to have 'God-esteem.' Not esteem for ourselves but esteem for God."

I liked that thought. And as I've worked on the ideas in this book, I've learned that in order to feel good about who I am, I have to know and trust the One who created me. It's only as I abide in Him—trusting Him, believing His Word, relying on Him—that I can have confidence and strength. And my confidence and strength will come from Him.

I'll see changes in me. But I'll recognize that they've come from Him and not from me. I can't do it. I can't change me. But

He can. He can change my thinking; He can change my outlook. Even changes like making time to exercise and to eat right can only happen (at least in my life!) through Him. I just don't have the strength.

Second Corinthians 3:5 sums up the idea of God-esteem perfectly. "Not that we are sufficient of ourselves to think of anything as being from ourselves, *but our sufficiency is from God*" (emphasis added). We are nothing without Him. All that we *do* or *say* or *are* comes from Him and can only come from Him as we grow in Him and daily build our relationship with Him.

That's been the key to my growth in Him from that very first moment when I came out of the woods on a new journey. I've given all to Him, and I'm trusting Him alone to lead me and guide me, now and until the end of my life. I will grow in confidence and courage as I grow in Him. Being His daughter gives me confidence. And God gave me a beautiful story that shows the confidence we can have when we're His daughters.

The palace was buzzing with activity. Tall guards lined the hallway. Light shone off them, filling the hallway with a golden glow. They were alert and strong. No one could enter the inner chamber without the guards knowing it. They watched intently—aware of every movement, of every person who passed by.

At the end of the massive hallway stood a huge doorway. The door was guarded by two immovable guards. The door itself was heavy. It was not made of wood but marble, and it had been polished till the light shone in it, its colors swirling in the creamy whiteness.

Through the door was the inner chamber, the throne room of the king. It was an incredible room. Huge, marble pillars framed the room. The walls were covered with a thick, purple cloth, such a deep purple that it almost seemed black; yet when the light shone on it, the color had such a depth that in itself it spoke of majesty and royalty. Gold and jewels decorated the walls. The floor shone. It, too, was made of marble; not the creamy white with the iridescent colors made by the light of the pillars and the door but shining white, so pure and clear it reflected all the colors of the gold and jewels and purple wall coverings.

The room was alive with people. Everyone had their purpose and was busy with their work. These people had important work to do. They ran the kingdom—every detail. Nothing kept them from seeing to their responsibilities. Nothing interrupted their attention to each detail.

In the center of the room sat the King. His eyes were gentle, yet they seemed to look into the very depth of your heart. His face was loving yet intent. He was intent on the work before Him. He made each decision and gave each order with wisdom and firmness. His features spoke of strength and might and power. The workers around Him spoke to Him with reverence and awe. They respected Him like no other. They would do anything for Him. *Anything.*

Down the hall came a noise. The guards stood at attention, ready to do whatever they needed to. Watching. Waiting. Those at the door stood their ground. No one would enter without permission.

The noise came closer. It was a little girl. She was skipping down the hall, not a care in the world. She didn't seem to be phased by the guards or the massive door ahead of her. She smiled and laughed and sang, headed for the doorway.

The guards saw her coming. They knew her. They let her pass, a smile on their faces. Those at the door relaxed their stance and opened the door for her to go through.

Inside the room, everyone looked up. They wanted to see who was coming in. Who was interrupting the work of the kingdom?

The King looked up too. His gentle eyes resting on the little girl. A smile broke wide on His face and lighted up the entire room. It spread to all the workers around Him, and each stopped their work. They smiled at the little girl. They watched and gathered around her as she approached the throne.

"Good morning, Father," she said, as she climbed up onto the King's lap.

"Good morning, Daughter, how glad I am to see you! I'm so glad you came to spend time with Me." Delight shone in the King's eyes. You could see the depth of love He had for His daughter. "Look, My daughter has come to see me," He told all the room.

As father and daughter spent time together, it was as if nothing else mattered. His eyes never left her face as she talked to Him, telling Him of her day, her cares, her struggles, her joys. The whole room listened. Nothing else mattered. Nothing else was as important as this time between father and daughter. No one else could just skip down the hall, past the guards, through the doorway, and stop all activity. People didn't just come uninvited.

But she had access to the King always. No matter what was happening, she was welcome to come in whenever she wanted to or needed Him. Everything stopped for her. Nothing was more important than she was to the King. She was His daughter.

You are the daughter. God is the King, the Father. You are always welcome in the court of heaven. God is never too busy. Nothing is more important than you. That's how great the Father's love is for you. That's how much He values you. When you pray to Him, you have His full attention. God listens. He cares. His eyes are full of love as they rest on you.

He wants you to have the confidence to live as His daughter, the confidence to trust Him with everything. He wants you to know Him. He's willing and waiting to reveal more and more of

Himself to you. He wants you to know Him only as a daughter can know her Father.

He will help you live as His daughter.

Reflection

1. What's the difference between self-sufficiency and God-sufficiency?
2. How can God's sufficiency help you to feel good and confident about who you are?
3. Picture yourself as God's daughter, His little girl. God gave me the picture in the story. What picture has He given you?

Prayer

Oh, Abba, Father, I just praise Your name. I can't comprehend what it really means to be Your daughter. Yours. You are my Father. You love me so incredibly. Help me to understand more of Your love, to rest confidently in that love, and to accept from You all that I need to make me feel that I belong, special, cared about. I love You, Lord. Help me to love You more. In Jesus' name, amen.